Process Theology and
the Christian Tradition

Studies in Historical Theology

Studies in Historical Theology
Volume V

Process Theology and the Christian Tradition

An Essay in Post Vatican II Thinking

Illtyd Trethowan
Monk of Downside Abbey

ST. BEDE'S PUBLICATIONS
Still River, Massachusetts

Imprimatur: Victor Farwell
Abbot President of the
English Benedictine Congregation

Worth Abbey
Crawley, Sussex
2 May 1984

The *Imprimatur* is an official declaration that a book or pamphlet is free of doctrinal and moral error. No implication is contained therein that the one granting the *Imprimatur* agrees with the content, opinions or statements expressed.

LIBRARY OF CONGRESS CATALOGING IN PUBLICATION DATA

Trethowan, Illtyd, 1907-
    Process theology and the Christian tradition.

    (Studies in historical theology)
    Includes index.
    1. Process theology.   I. Title.   II. Series: Studies in historical
theology (Still River, Mass.)
BT83.6.T74   1985   230   84-26240
ISBN 0-932506-36-4

To
Rex Tomlinson
in gratitude
for his encouragement

Contents

Introduction

This essay is not written primarily for specialists or for highly educated general readers, although there are some footnotes for their possible interest, but for anyone who takes process theology seriously enough to consider reading a book which criticizes it. It is not an affair of clever argument or logical expertise or the assembly of historical facts. Anyone can understand what is going on who is prepared to stop and think, to *ponder* the considerations offered. It is not necessary to have read very much in order to do this. I avoid technical terms unless they are really useful, in which case I explain them. But it may be necessary to have some means of distinguishing between what makes religious *sense* and what does not; and that seems to depend largely on religious practice, in particular on the sort of praying which is not confined to public worship and other social activities. There are people who are far advanced in this sort of prayer and are therefore, fundamentally, far more intelligent (as distinct from being clever) than the rest of us, while their vocabulary remains very limited. I shall be trying to avoid not only unexplained technical words but also unusual ones, but I may be told by the typist that my notion of the 'usual' has given her many good laughs. Nevertheless I shall go on trying.

The subtitle seemed forced upon me because I wanted to indicate with the required brevity that, although I reject the fundamental contention of the process theologians (that God has two 'poles', at one of which he is perfect and at the other in process of development) and am therefore what is called in this context a 'traditionalist', I am not the sort of 'traditionalist' who supposes that the Christian tradition became immobilized early in this century or at some time in the last one or, in extreme cases, at the Council of Trent. (I shall refer to the Christian tradition simply as 'the tradition' when the context precludes ambiguity.) The fundamental contention of the process thinkers might not sound at first hearing as though it mattered much, but it leads to conclusions which are obviously opposed to historic Christianity: for instance, life with God after death for ourselves as individual persons is no part of its normal programme. In a way, though, I welcome it; its practitioners cause Christians to think about things which they badly need to think about, and sometimes, I hope, to learn things from them that are well worth learning. Indeed it is an excellent thing that process theology should have aroused so wide an interest, *provided* that something better is also visibly on offer. And the very fact that it can be a menace to Christians should encourage people, as it has encouraged me, to put the case for the other side in a way which may prove useful. Process thinkers seem, on the whole, to be strangely ignorant of post-Vatican II theology and might be expected to read an example of it referring directly to them.

Theology in the (Roman) Catholic Church before Vatican II had been for long in a generally frozen state.[1] Roman theologians had imposed standard opinions on the faithful as though they were bound up with the faith. There are still plenty of people around who suppose themselves called upon to believe certain doctrines of which they have no understanding and which prove, in fact, not to be understandable. At one time they were able to accept these as 'mysteries', meaning by this that they appeared to make no sense but that the authorities of the Church had been empowered somehow to assure us of their truth. It becomes important for such Catholics to realize that their theologians have been moving away for some time from fossilized ideas (more slowly than elsewhere, naturally enough, in the Congregation for the Defence of the Faith)

---

[1]Gabriel Daly's *Transcendence and Immanence,* (Oxford, 1980) is instructive on this.

to traditional ones which had gone, more or less, underground and that a theological 'mystery' is something to which all the faithful are supposed to have some clue, although—since it is about God—we can never get our minds *round* it. To take an important instance of the change which has taken place, although it is no special concern of process thinkers, there is a view of the Redemption still current in both Catholic and Reformed circles, according to which the sufferings and death of Jesus Christ were accepted by God quite literally *in exchange* for the remission of all men's sins. This sort of language is found in the Bible and therefore in the liturgy, but it seems plain to people who think about it nowadays that it can be no more than a rhetorical way of saying that Jesus Christ gained new life for himself and for us *through* (at the 'cost' of) his death—his final act of self-giving love. Children are regularly taught nowadays, in some parts of the world at least, that we are united, if we are willing, with the risen life of Jesus, and empowered thereby to rise from our sins.[2] The 'cost' of his death was not something paid over as a recompense to God. People used to talk of 'the demands of God's justice'. But what sort of God would that be?

So questions raised by process thinkers have to be seen against the background of this whole developing situation. Tradition, as book after book has been insisting for many years past, is not the dead weight which process thinkers so often inveigh against but the Church's continuing life, although sometimes it seems dormant and for the time being this or that aspect of it can be almost lost to sight. The Church's critics make fun sometimes of her belief that she is guided by the Holy Spirit: 'just look at what actually happens to her', they say, 'is *that* the Holy Spirit's work?' No, indeed, but the Holy Spirit does not bring force to bear on us; he will guide our minds, but only if we let him. It is well to remember that there have been times when the Church seemed to be heading for dissolution and then the situation was gradually transformed by the appearance of

[2]See F. X. Durrwell's *The Resurrection*, (Sheed and Ward, 1960).

a few great saints in unlikely quarters. Could *they* have 'quenched the Spirit' then? Certainly they *might* have done so. But what in fact they proceeded to do is some evidence for his being always around.

Here I must refer to certain popular misconceptions about the debate between process thinkers and 'traditionalist' ones (or between 'neo-classical' and 'classical' ones). A casual observer might receive the impression that it is just a debate between Catholics and Protestants. In fact process theology has never had any necessary connection with Christianity (except for purposes of criticizing traditional views about God), and there are Catholics who accept its points of view to a greater or a lesser extent. Nor is it just a debate between Thomists and non-Thomists. Moreover by 'Thomism' is often meant in this context that travesty of the thought of St Thomas Aquinas which was in most places until some twenty years ago the standard fare of Catholic higher education. It seems to me that there is a great deal of truth in what St Thomas wrote and that it would be a great mistake to disregard it, but I am unable to accept certain of his main principles. To suppose that process thought is a passing American fashion is another misconception. It is more than half a century old and shows signs of spreading beyond its country of origin. What American Christians think (especially, I would say, American Catholics) is going to have great importance for the world at large. It may be useful for an English Catholic who has sympathy with a number of positions typically held by process thinkers to say plainly and in some detail why he regards process thinking as an insufficient basis for religion and, in particular, for traditional Catholic theology. The topic is broached in the first chapter.

Process theology is little known in Europe (but interest in it is growing, in England at least), so I have explained its central doctrines (with which alone I am concerned) by quoting extensively from leading process thinkers. I have quoted extensively also from Father W. Norris Clarke's important book *The Philosophical Approach to God* and make grateful acknowledgement of the help which it has given me.

Process Theology and
the Christian Tradition

I
Basic Ideas

In 1977 a book was published by the Westminster Press, *Process Theology—An Introductory Exposition* by John B. Cobb, Jr. and David Ray Griffin; it was republished in the United Kingdom by Christian Journals Limited of Belfast the following year. It would seem that it has been widely accepted as representative of process thought, and so it will be the basis for discussion at the outset.

The founder of process thought was Alfred North Whitehead, an Englishman who was born in 1861 and taught mathematics at the University of London until his acceptance of a chair of philosophy at Harvard. His major works belong to the twenties and thirties of this century; they are sometimes obscure and there are controversies about their interpretation, but I shall be concerned only with certain major issues which are clear enough. His successor was Charles Hartshorne, who has been writing books on process theology for more than fifty years and with whom the theory of a 'dipolar' God is nowadays specially associated.

Cobb and Griffin devote their first chapter to an account of Whitehead's 'basic philosophical ideas'. The first is that 'to be *actual* is to be a process'; anything else is 'an abstraction from process, not a full-fledged actuality'. The passage continues:

> The bare assertion that the actual is processive has religious significance even by itself. Since the world as we experience it is a place of process, of change, of becoming, of growth and decay, the contrary notion that what is actual or fully real is beyond change leads to a devaluation of life in the world. Since

our basic religious drive is to be in harmony with the fully real,
belief that the fully real is beyond process encourages one or
another form of escape from full participation in the world.
But to understand that process is the reality directs the drive
to be 'with it' into immersion in the process.[1]

That sums up most conveniently the general attitude of
process thinkers. Belief in a changeless God, perfect and
infinite, is supposed to lead to a lack of interest in what
goes on in the world. (The lives of the Christian saints
do not bear out this supposition.) Religion is simply a
matter of plunging oneself into what one regards as the
proper development of this world. There seems to be the
suggestion that traditional believers regard the world as
somehow unreal, since they are supposed to think that
only God is 'fully real'. But that was probably not intended.
Our authors go on at once to claim that their views are
consonant with the Christian tradition because in it 'God
has been viewed as active within the historical process'.
The question remains whether he has any reality apart
from it. It cannot be denied that the notion of a God who is
himself in process of development is alien not only to the
Christian tradition but to the vast majority of contemporary believers in God, whether Christian or not. And, so
far as one can make out, this is not the way in which
religion has been normally understood in earlier ages.[2]

The next idea of Whitehead's to be mentioned is that of
the time-process as a 'transition' from one actual entity to
another. These are 'momentary events'. What we ordinarily call an event consists, for Whitehead, in a great many
'events' in his sense of the term. These have 'a unity of
their own' and are 'momentary experiences', usually called
'actual occasions' or 'occasions of experience'; they are the
only 'true individuals'. Our own personal experience is a
'serially-ordered society of such occasions', which are
themselves processes; for 'they are not to be understood as

---

[1] P. 14.

[2] On this *Understanding Religion,* (Duckworth, 1983) by E. J. Sharpe is
useful.

things that endure through a tiny bit of time unchanged, but as taking that bit of time to become'.[3] That process is what Whitehead calls 'concrescence'. This, our authors say, 'opens the way for a variety of religious experiences'. For it 'establishes the importance of time' and 'the experience of the eternal "now" is also intelligible' because 'the successiveness of transition does not apply' to concrescence itself.[4] These remarks are made, presumably, with Eastern mysticism in mind. Both Eastern and Christian mystics would be surprised to hear that the timelessness of individual moments might explain their sublime experiences. And the question arises whether, on this account, there can be a continuing 'self', a subject capable of union with God.

Now we come to Whitehead's idea of 'enjoyment':

> Every unit of process, whether at the level of the human or of electronic events, has enjoyment. Hence we are not to think of enjoyment as being necessarily conscious, or as related to the pleasure end of the pleasure-pain continuum. What we normally mean by pleasure is bound up not only with consciousness but with the whole structure of high-grade animal bodies. But we can distinguish within this rich matrix of meaning an element that can be broadly generalized. To be, to actualize oneself, to act upon others, to share in a wider community, is to enjoy being an experiencing subject quite apart from any accompanying pain or pleasure.[5]

Does it make sense to say that electronic events can enjoy 'being an experiencing subject', unless we suppose that they are in some degree conscious? Whitehead, we learn, held that 'only a few experiences rise to the level of consciousness'; he 'rejects a (Cartesian) dualism of experiencing and non-experiencing actualities'.[6] I must confess to making nothing of this.

[3]P. 15.
[4]Pp. 15-16.
[5]Pp. 16-17.
[6]P. 17. Descartes' distinction between mind and body is not the only possible one. Can one deny that there is one?

Our authors tell us that 'a momentary experience is essentially related to previous experiences...it begins as a multiplicity of relations and achieves its individuality through its relation to and unification of those relations'. We naturally ask how 'a multiplicity of relations' can constitute anything. The rest of the passage may not throw much light on that, but it is useful as giving a context for two important Whiteheadian expressions: 'It [the "experience" or "occasion"] is not first something in itself, which only secondarily enters into relations with others. The relations are primary. Whitehead's technical terms for these relations are "prehension" and "feeling". The present occasion is nothing but its process of unifying the particular prehensions with which it begins'.[7] The reader may be left with the impression that something is both present in a sort of a way and absent in a sort of a way at the same time. I think that he will be right. Whitehead is talking about self-creation, bringing oneself into existence. And then you have to be already there to do it, or so it seems to me.

We also hear that 'the next molecular occasion within that series constituting the enduring molecule, or the next moment of human experience within that stream of experiences constituting the soul, is open to the contributions that can be received from others'.[8] This suggests an account of the 'self' which would make it more permanent than it has so far seemed to be. What follows continues to suggest this: 'In such a stream of occasions, a "defining essence" of that stream may arise, representing the characteristics which apply to each member of the stream'. But it is then repeated that this is 'an abstraction in comparison with the individual occasions themselves, which alone are fully concrete individuals'. A little later, however, we read that 'ethical independence as a characteristic of ourselves as enduring persons is still a positive idea...it is good not

[7]Pp. 19-20.
[8]P. 20.

to be swayed from ethical principles by changing circumstances'.[9] So it is all rather baffling.

'Incarnation' is the heading for the next topic, which proves to be largely about memory. In memory the past 'lives on objectively, as objectified and hence incarnated in the present'. It is the object, in other words, of a new experience, not an old experience persisting or being renewed. And 'since our activities will make a difference throughout the future...influence as incarnation implies that we will be objectively immortal'.[10] It may be agreeable to think of one's future influence upon the world, but if we ourselves are going to be snuffed out it seems cold comfort. The past, however, 'does not dictate precisely how it will be immortalized...each actuality is partially self-creative; it finally creates itself out of the material that is given to it'.[11] There is nothing to suggest that it is given by God and we might suppose that he has faded out of the picture, but in the next page he comes into it again in a big way: 'The divine reality so relates to us as to heighten the probability that enjoyment will be enhanced. The individual experience finally determines, within the limits made possible by God and the world, what enjoyment it will realise'. The next paragraph, explaining this, demands quotation in full:

> Although God's role is in this way like that of other aspects of the environment, it also has its uniqueness. The aim of enjoyment is not simply one among many aspects of an experience. It is the one element in terms of which the entity achieves its unity. This aim is not derived from the past world, for it is unique to the new occasion. The attractive possibility, the lure, in relation to which its act of self-determination is made, is derived from God. This lure is called 'the initial aim'.

[9]P. 22.
[10]P. 23. P. 124 shows that life after death is no normal tenet of process theology.
[11]P. 25.

God is the divine Eros urging the world to new heights of enjoyment.[12]

So Whitehead's God is the revealer of opportunities and the stimulus to seizing upon them. Our fulfilment is not seen to be in God himself. Nevertheless the idea that he is always offering what is best for us should surely be part of any Christian account of providence. (This should not be taken to mean that God arranges disasters as a means of furthering his beneficent designs.)

We now come to a particularly remarkable passage: 'The doctrine that every occasion of experience aims at its own self-creation points to only one-half of its creative aim. Equally essential is the occasion's aim to pervade the environment, i.e., to be creative of the future... an occasion of experience in creating itself does not aim solely at its own private enjoyment; it also aims to create itself in such a way as to make a definite contribution to the future'.[13] This seems to be saying that the world's development proceeds without check or hindrance: there is no problem of evil. It does not help much to be told just after this that one of the 'religious implications' of this doctrine is that, because 'the concern for the future is a variable... it can be enlarged and strengthened'.[14] So progress, it is admitted, is not always going on. This enlargement and strengthening is then said to be 'the function of morality, which is, therefore, important for God's purposes in the world'. What Christians call 'sin' would seem to be reduced to a series of minor hitches which can hold things up a bit. I am reminded of Christopher Dawson's remark that some missionary saint was martyred 'by rather slack Christians'.

Our authors have said earlier that 'efficient causation', which is the activity of one actuality upon another, is

[12]P. 26. The technical terms 'the subjective aim', 'the initial aim', and 'the lure' are in regular use.

[13]Pp. 26-27.

[14]P. 27. Later in the book the authors speak of moral evil in Christian terms.

by means of 'entering into' the other.[15] This is not the way in which I should speak of God's causing the world, but, apart from that, I welcome in general principle the opening of their first chapter's last section ('God-Relatedness'): 'What has been said of the divine incarnation in the world, the derivation from God of the initial aim towards enjoyment, and God as the organ of novelty, shows that the prehension of God is an essential part of all experience'. They also say here: 'If we could think at all of a world apart from God, it would be a world of repetitions lapsing into lesser and lesser forms of order according to the principle of entropy'.[16] Apparently there is a principle of progressive decline which God, as it were, finds on stage waiting to be coped with. And this brings to the centre of our attention for the first time something which has been already implicit in this account of Whitehead's ideas: for process theology, God is not the creator in the ordinary sense of the word—he finds himself faced by an eternal world in a state of original chaos. But it is not until the fourth chapter of this book that this is plainly stated and then briefly:

> Process theology rejects the notion of *creation ex nihilo*, if that means out of *absolute* nothingness. That doctrine is part and parcel of the doctrine of God as absolute controller. Process theology affirms instead a doctrine of creation out of chaos (which was suggested not only by Plato, but also by more Old Testament passages than the doctrine of creation out of nothing). A state of absolute chaos would be one in which there is nothing but very low-grade occasions happening at random, i.e., without being ordered into enduring individuals.[17]

So Whitehead's God persuades the 'occasions' to let him order them, for we have found that they too have an initiative and must freely do their part. Discussion might seem called for here, but we now pass to an account of the

[15]P. 23.
[16]P. 29.
[17]P. 65.

evolutionary process in terms of electrons, protons, and so forth.

Most people are startled when they hear for the first time that Plato's description of creation in the *Timaeus* is seriously put forward by contemporary academics, especially when the Old Testament is adduced as an authority for it. Father W. Norris Clarke, S.J., in his impressive book *The Philosophical Approach to God*[18] has written that 'practically all of the great metaphysicians of the past, East and West, except Plato and Aristotle, have agreed on at least this: that every man must ultimately be grounded in some more primordial One' and that 'what is missing from Whiteheadian metaphysics is that it remains content with Plato's Demiurge without passing on to the underlying doctrine of the One or the Good, which Plato himself finally saw had to be the last word and which Plotinus carried all the way to its implicit consequences—the origin of matter from the One'.[19] Clarke observes that, in Whitehead's system, 'the individual bursts of self-creativity which characterize each newly arising actual entity... seem literally to emerge out of nothing'.[20] Referring to theologians who regard this system as compatible with Christianity, and with particular reference to John Cobb, Clarke touches on their claim that God's gift of the 'initial subjective aim of each new actual occasion' might be considered as 'an initial gift of being' and points out that 'we would still be faced with the emergence out of nothing of the entity's actuality as an actual power'.[21] Nor does the claim alter the fact that God is at best a co-creator on this view: on any showing, his operations presuppose some sort of existing universe. Clarke also points out that 'creativity for Whitehead is not an actuality in and for itself but...seems to be an ultimate primordial *many*, with no unifying source'.[22] He rubs this in by saying that, in

---

[18]Published by Wake Forest University, 1979.

[19]*Op. cit.*, p. 75.

[20]P. 73.

[21]P. 76.

[22]P. 72.

Whitehead's system, 'the many has radical priority, since the duality of God *and* world . . . is itself an ultimate original many'.[23]

What, then, is the Christian tradition's 'basic idea' in this matter? How is our knowledge of God supposed to originate? Does it result from a reasoning process based on indisputable facts? Many people seem to think this the only possible way of vindicating theism. Before taking up this question we may usefully remind ourselves that there are plenty of people around who are content with an 'ultimate original many'. I have pointed out above that to talk of 'self-creation' is self-contradictory. But it is not self-contradictory to say that things 'just happen'. It is only to say that the world in which we find ourselves is one of which we can make no sense. This is indeed a position which may prove an uncomfortable one, but it is at least not obvious how anyone can be *argued* out of it. Are there, then, to repeat, any solid arguments *for* a creator of this world? No, if by a 'solid argument' is meant what Father Clarke refers to as 'the type of formal-logical argument that can (if indeed any argument for anything real can) force the mind to accept it with compelling logical rigor'.[24] He might seem to suggest that if you want to find out whether something *exists*, you must have your own evidence for it, somehow come in contact with it, unless you have information about it from some wholly trustworthy person who claims to have had contact with it—and people who demand 'solid' proof are not likely to accept such a claim. It would not follow that all arguments for God are useless; some may have a certain plausibility and may arouse a certain interest. So there will be a brief discussion of the so-called traditional arguments, the 'Five Ways' of St Thomas Aquinas, which is also requisite because it is so often supposed that 'traditionalists' are committed to them. In fact the Christian tradition is not committed to the philosophy of any one thinker or school.

[23]P. 74.
[24]P. 38.

St Thomas's 'Five Ways' summarize very briefly the arguments offered by pagan philosophers, Aristotle in particular; he does not appear to attach special importance to them (philosophy was important for him only because faith must be shown to harmonize with natural reason and may be prepared for by it—which is not to say that he did not also *enjoy* philosophizing). His first three arguments, each in its own fashion, conclude that our world could not have brought itself into existence and that therefore there must be a creator of it: the fourth, about 'degrees of perfection', is usually regarded by Thomists as depending for such efficacy as it may have on the previous ones (it raises the very pertinent question: where do our *ideals* come from?). The fifth, the so called 'argument from design' (in fact an argument *for* design) appeals to the presence of order in the world as evidence for a designer. Whitehead's argument is a form of it: there must be some beneficent being capable of 'luring' the world to richer and richer forms of life. But this argument, even if it were unanswerable, would give us only a super-architect, not God's infinite perfection. Clarke writes about the 'Five Ways': 'First of all, I consider them in their actual textual form to be very poorly adapted to convince the ordinary modern thinker. Second, I do not think that they represent St Thomas's own truly original and most characteristic metaphysical structure of ascent to God as shown in the rest of his works'.[25] There are Thomists who regard it as quite unreasonable to reject the argument for a First Cause of the world if one accepts that events within the world-order do not occur without some reason. But it is difficult to attribute such rejection just to stupidity and obstinacy; there is the problem of evil (to which we shall turn in a later connection) to be balanced against an undemonstrative, ineffective argument. And, to repeat, it is always possible to fall back on saying 'things just happen'. But the claims made by Clarke for the 'structure of ascent' which he calls the 'most direct of all metaphysical arguments for God'

[25]P. 35.

deserve to be weighed. 'Its power', he writes, 'perhaps lies more in the evocation of a basic metaphysical insight which is then laid out in the form of an argument.... It may be too that the efficacy of the argument is so inextricably involved in a profound existential commitment of the living dynamism of the spirit to a truly personal quest for the full intelligibility of the universe that it can remain opaque if one stands back in a purely detached, abstract, logical perspective'.[26] In other words, since the argument does not possess 'logical rigor', some other factor in the situation must be brought in to make up for it. Does a 'commitment' to a 'quest' fill the bill?

Earlier in his book Father Clarke has moved towards an answer which seems to me both simpler and more profound. He is discussing with sympathy the 'Transcendental Thomists', of whom Rahner and Lonergan are probably the best known. He writes that 'they rejoined in a new way the old Augustinian inner way to God' and that 'they brought out of obscurity into full development St Thomas's own profound doctrine of the dynamism of the human spirit'.[27] Unfortunately, as it seems to me, they did so in needlessly complicated language which has made

---

[26]P. 38. Father Clarke quotes on the next page 'one of St Thomas's own succinct versions' of the argument from the *De Potentia*, q. 3, a. 5. 'It is necessary that if some one attribute is found in common among many things, it be caused in them by some one cause. For it cannot be said that this common attribute belongs to each one as derived from its own self (*ex se ipso*), since each one, according as it is its own unique self, is distinguished from every other, and a diversity of causes produces a diversity of effects. Therefore since the act of existence (*esse*) is found common to all things (shared by all things), which, according to *what* they are, are distinct from each other, it must be that their act of existence is communicated to them not from themselves but from some one cause. And that seems to be the reasoning of Plato, who maintained that before all multiplicity there is a unity, not only in numbers but in real things'. It seems to me that an *apprehension* of the One in the many is necessary if this is to be accepted. Talking to an 'ordinary modern thinker' about an 'act of existence' is not likely to get one anywhere.

[27]P. 16.

their views inaccessible to the general reading public. It has often been objected that they concentrate on the movement ('dynamism') of the intellect towards God rather than on its function of *uniting* us with him. But eventually Clarke speaks plainly of 'the unveiling, the uncovering *within* us, of the God who has always already been there, existentially drawing us to Himself, but not yet recognized as such'.[28] Making this implicit awareness explicit, he here remarks, may 'involve much intellectual discussion and groping'. All that it really needs, I would say, is that sort of *attention* which leads to prayer.[29] But I have a disappointment later when Clarke proves to regard the 'inner way' as giving us not 'the knowledge of God *as Creator of all things*' but only the knowledge of him as 'goal'.[30] Our total dependence on God for our continued existence and the same total dependence of the world on him can be recognized, I would say, together. That, in the end, I think, is what has to be said to Whiteheadians.

It might seem that I have been wandering off into irrelevant disputes. But the 'Transcendental Thomists' are well-known, at least in some circles, and it was necessary to indicate where I differ from them. And Father Clarke's standing is such that I must give my reasons for not following him at all points (here I must add that I am greatly indebted to his various writings). We shall be returning to *A Philosophical Approach to God* for help in later chapters. A discussion of the philosophical 'proofs' seemed, in the circumstances, the necessary preliminary to a statement about Christian belief in God, as it did to St Thomas (who, far from leaving God a remote abstraction at the end of a syllogism, goes on to speak of our union with him in the order of grace, the object of his whole exercise). But the central concern of the Christian tradition is theological, God's revelation of himself in Jesus Christ and the new life

---

[28]P. 26.

[29]Anyone who thinks it odd to mention prayer in connection with the philosophy of religion might turn to the works of Gabriel Marcel.

[30]Pp. 33-34. This is the point at which Father Clarke moves on to St Thomas's 'structure of ascent' to God.

which Jesus has made available for us by his passage
through this world, culminating in his death and resurrection. Christian faith is something more than a rational
conviction that these beliefs are true; it implies a conscious
relationship with God in Jesus, with Jesus as our way
to God.[31] How one can come to knowledge of God is a
philosophical question on which the tradition has nothing
definitive to say beyond the claim that the natural human
reason *can* come to such a knowledge. I would put the point
like this: God's offer to us must be addressed to us in our
natural condition before we can gain through our acceptance of it that personal, 'supernatural', relationship with
him in love as well as knowledge that goes by the name of
grace. We can find this offer addressed to us when we find
God present to our minds. If I had announced this thesis
about God's presence at the outset there would have been
less chance, I thought, of its gaining a hearing than if I let it
emerge gradually in the course of discussing the 'proofs'. It
will prove to explain a curious situation which presented
itself during the discussion. But first I must try to defend
the thesis briefly and to indicate both that it has had a long
history and that it is a live option at the present time.

God is active everywhere, but only some of his creatures
can be aware of his activity. Awareness is an experience,
the basic form of knowledge, mental contact with what is
other than ourselves. Through our awareness of our own
bodies in the changes which take place in them (that is, in
our sense-organs) we become aware of other bodies which
affect them. We know these bodies *in* knowing our own:
the cause is known *in* the effect. At the same time we
become aware of our own mental activity, of our mental
powers, of our *selves*. And in these we can find God. That, as
I see it, is the 'basic idea', the basis for the 'inner way' to
God known as Augustinian, although the record of it goes
back indefinitely before St Augustine. It is a Platonic
rather than an Aristotelian way, and it turns up regularly
in the Christian mystical tradition (Christianity is not just

[31]To this I shall return.

a 'moralism'), in the Fathers, in the Middle Ages with St Bonaventure, then with Pascal, Newman, and, in our own century, Maurice Blondel, to mention only a few of the great names.

Like other contemporary thinkers, I call our awareness of God a direct but *mediate* one. It happens in a medium, that of the knowledge of the self and its environment. *In ourselves* and what surrounds us we find that there is a 'beyond', not only in the sense that our field of knowledge is limited but also in the sense that, if we *attend*, there is something invisible to the eye but pressing, as it were, on the edge of the mind, supporting it and filling it with a vague hope. It can suggest to us an idea of perfection which will prove to be that of an absolute love, a pure generosity. Or it may suggest to us in the first instance the idea of unlimited beauty. It may also suggest to us that idea of perfect intelligibility, perfect understanding, which, as the 'Transcendental Thomists' say, can be verified only in God. But I suspect that those of us who are not academics (as were those whom Father Clarke was addressing) would not find that that came home to us at once. What is at first only an idea can declare itself, given time and patience, to be the truth. It can even do so without any apparent preliminaries.

It is, I think, in our moral experience that, for most people, God is most readily recognizable. The *value* which we respect in persons especially but also in the world at large, our freedom to promote or to disregard it, our moral responsibility, is not easy to account for on any other showing. (To put it all down to the influence of society upon us is the only live alternative, and to me at least it seems wholly implausible.) Why should it seem to most people, even those who disclaim any interest in religion, that to go against one's conscience is somehow to attack one's own nature? Why should people 'sacrifice themselves' for the sake of others unless life has a purpose, a destiny, to which we are all committed? Why should we have 'rights' if we differ from other animals only in having more brain-power? Such questions can lead to the discovery that, as Pascal said, God is always known but seldom recognized. What was thought of before as a *duty* is still there, but transformed into the Good, the heart's desire. And then a number of things start coming together. We can see how God has never left himself without witness, how people in all times and places can have answered his call unknowingly by giving joy to others and relieving distress, so linking themselves with him. In all self-forgetful activity, in all acceptance of absolute claims on one, the unrecognized God is worshipped. Then it can be discovered that all awareness of the *other* is a form of *union*, the touch, however slight, of the other upon the subject, changing it, if only a little, while remaining itself unchanged, without intermediary or distortion, because it is a fore-shadowing of our union with God.

The curious situation (mentioned above) which arose in the discussion of the proofs was that an argument admittedly not simply a matter of logic should never-theless seem to become acceptable in virtue of a 'basic metaphysical insight'. An 'insight' into the principle of causality, revealing its validity for our purposes, could be, so far as I can see, only the discovery that talking about 'the principle of causality' is really talking (though somewhat oddly) about God. Then the 'basic metaphysical insight' which the argument was supposed to 'evoke' can be nothing but the discovery of God's universal presence. So the argument is not backing up or being backed up by the insight but is simply superseded by it, although this does not make all argument useless. A causal argument can 'evoke' the discovery of God: it asks a question to which the answer has been given already but not adverted to, and the answer can then be attributed to the (supposed) force of the argument. To put this into more concrete terms, people who are told that the causal argument is not logically sound will sometimes say 'there must be a creator; it is unthinkable that there should not be', supposing that this *must* is somehow a logical one. It seems clear to me that what it really means is that a dim awareness of God has sufficiently grown for a conviction to be formed, although it is still not recognized for what it is. There *must* be a creator, then, because I cannot get him out of my mind. The cause is present *in* the effect, not 'proved' *by* it. Yet apologists go on saying that some arguments for Christianity cannot be 'seen' until one has 'faith'. What this really means, I suggest, is that some arguments are not shown to be reaching the right conclusion until other arguments have been added to give them support (in which case they may acquire a certain validity for practical purposes and one has a 'practical' faith in them) or that a fresh factor, the awareness of Christian faith, has transformed the situation. In neither case can the arguments *of themselves* be 'seen', recognized as valid.

In an article published a few years ago, H. P. Owen, Professor of Christian Doctrine at King's College, University of London, wrote as follows:

> It seems to me clear that rational demonstration is neither the way in which in fact we know that God exists nor a means by which it is possible to know it. That Christians at any rate do not in fact come to know God thus is shown by the Bible which bases this knowledge wholly on a direct, though mediated, apprehension of God's personal presence.... Within Christianity, when it first occurs or recurs in some specially cogent way, it usually takes the form (classically expressed by Augustine) of discovering that God has always been with us even if we have not always been with him.[32]

That may allay the suspicions of some readers who may have found these views unusual and surprising. But there are also Catholics who have been brought up to suppose that talk about 'experience of God' is frowned upon by their authorities not only when it refers to emotional states which have no evidential value but also when there are claims of a directness of any sort about the way in which we gain knowledge of God. I shall discuss in some

---

[32]'God and Moral Obligation', *The Downside Review*, July 1977, pp. 195, 197. Owen then quotes some less authoritative statements to the same effect from several books of mine, of which *Mysticism and Theology*, (London, Geoffrey Chapman, 1975) is probably the most accessible.

detail at the end of this book the change of attitude which has occurred in this regard among orthodox Catholics during the past half-century. But it may be useful at once to refer to a little book published in 1981 by Father Dermot Lane, *The Experience of God*, with the promising subtitle 'An Invitation to do Theology' (and with the Archbishop of Dublin's *imprimatur*). This too I shall discuss in some detail later. Lane, though his vocabulary differs from mine, will be seen to be in fundamental agreement with me by the following passage:

> The central point here is that the presence of God in the world, communicated through the religious dimension of human experience, is neither a presence directly available only to a privileged few nor a presence mediated simply through logical deduction to the learned. [But what sort of 'presence' *could* that be?] Instead the reality of God in the world is a presence that is accessible to all; it is that gracious omnipresence in which every human being 'lives, moves and has his being' whether it is consciously recognized or not. One of the primary tasks of theology today is how to make the individual experientially present to God. [33]

This chapter will end with a few comments on the second chapter of *Process Theology—An Introductory Exposition* in which Cobb and Griffin complete what they have to say about Whitehead's 'basic ideas'. I am happy to agree, in principle, with their first thesis: 'One's conscious beliefs may conflict with what is "known" at the pre-reflective level'. They instance the belief that what is called 'efficient causation' is in fact no more than 'constant conjunction' although 'the experience of causation as real influence cannot be effaced'. And this, they add, 'holds for such other elements of pre-reflective experience as self-determination and God-relatedness'. [34] ('Self-determination', which a Christian reader might suppose to refer simply to our freedom of

---

[33]Pp. 16-17. The book is available from Veritas Publications, Dublin. Twelve of its eighty-seven pages are filled with references to writers supporting the author's positions.

[34]*Op. cit.*, p. 31.

choice, must be taken here as referring generally to 'self-creativity'.) It does not follow that conscious beliefs are unimportant, for 'to the extent that our conscious beliefs are in tension with universal features of human experience, we are split within ourselves'.[35] But 'whether we consciously believe in efficient causation or not, our total life-stance will still reflect our pre-reflective knowledge of its reality'. An important passage follows:

> The same holds true for our experience of deity. We all know, at the pre-reflective level, that there is a sacred reality, whose existence is supremely valuable, and that our lives finally have meaning because of our relation to this holy reality. This knowledge conditions the emotions, attitudes and actions even of those who affirm atheism and nihilism. Further, we all feel the impulse to be the best we can in each moment, and to contribute the most we can to the future. This is reflected in the lives even of those who reject all teleological notions [those of a purpose in the world], all ideas of objective values and all moral principles.[36]

This shows how much ground is common to Christian process thinkers and traditional Christians. It strikes a deeper note than is usual in this literature, it demands one's sincere respect, but it seems to gloss over, as did a passage previously quoted, the existence in the world of *moral evil* and its dire results. The awareness of God does not grow automatically in the human mind: his presence has to be responded to, if only in the anonymous form of 'conscience'. No doubt there are many people who reject all theories of 'conscience' but are truly 'conscientious' all the same. But all the evidence goes to show that there are many (perhaps many more than there used to be) whose motives are largely those of greed and hatred.

Some of Whitehead's views on religion are then usefully explained. 'Religious doctrines claiming universal validity are to be accepted, if at all, because of their self-evidence'.[37]

[35]P. 34.
[36]P. 32.
[37]P. 36.

We might suppose that they would be very few indeed. But we are told: 'Referring to these doctrines as self-evidently true does not mean that they are equally obvious to everyone. On the contrary. The ability to perceive the previously unformulated factors in experience is extremely rare.... The point is that, once someone has perceived them consciously and expressed them verbally, they can then be recognized by others'. It follows from this that 'theology should not primarily be argumentation. It should primarily be the attempt to state the basic tenets of one's faith in such a way as to elicit a responsive perception of these as self-evidently true'.[38] Nothing in all this is considered an objection to Christianity's 'necessary reference to historical events'. Cobb and Griffin declare: 'We have faith in the continued fruitfulness of returning to the first accounts of and reactions to Jesus' life for new insights because of the repeated fruitfulness of this return in the past'.[39] Necessarily I have been quoting for the most part passages from their book with which I disagree. I hope to have suggested here that Christians may find much in it to accept and to applaud. But I must take issue with it again in the next chapter.

[38] P. 37.
[39] P. 40.

II
Charges Against the Tradition

This book is not only a cursory critique of process theology from a traditional Christian point of view but also an account of some features of the tradition which have been, and in some quarters still are, largely ignored. So in the previous chapter as much time was spent in outlining a traditional approach to the question of God's reality as in outlining Whitehead's approach to it. And in the present chapter process theology's positions, according to Professors Cobb and Griffin, involving its main charges against the tradition, must be commented on and compared with a further series of traditional standpoints which seem to be curiously overlooked. There is, inevitably, an unsatisfactoriness about this piecemeal procedure, but it may be considered as putting together the elements of a traditional system of thought to be exhibited eventually as a whole. The third chapter in Cobb and Griffin which, apart from a few references to the fourth, is the last which we have to deal with, begins by way of a general introduction with a section headed 'The Existence of God', and in it 'the movement of Whitehead's thought to God' is thus indicated:

> He envisions a vast congeries of events coming into being momentarily and then lapsing into the past. Each new event must take account of the many events that make up the world for it. It must do so in some definite way, for without definiteness there is no actuality. Since it has a past different from that of any event in its world, it must have a new form of definiteness. The past cannot impose such a form on it, since the present can derive from the past only what the past

contains. This form of definiteness can be derived only from the sphere of possibility. But the sphere of possibility is purely abstract, lacking all agency to provide selectivity for the need of new events. There must be an agency that mediates between these abstract forms or pure possibilities and the actual world. This agency is best conceived as an envisage-ment of the abstract forms of definiteness such as to establish their graded relevance to every new situation in the actual world.[1]

The 'agency', as we have already seen, is Whitehead's God (a philosopher's God, as this passage conveniently indicates, rather than the God of religion), who 'lures' the world to actualize fresh possibilities. What the passage particularly brings home to us is that this 'sphere of possi-bility' has some shadowy existence which Whitehead's God finds waiting for him just as he finds the 'void' waiting for him as material for his beneficent operations. It is all the more surprising to find on the same page: 'A theistic vision of all reality can gain adherence best by displaying its superior adequacy to other visions'. For what emerges most importantly from my first chapter is that the God of process theology has not the same claims on our worship as the God who is Alpha and Omega, the source of every-one and everything to whom all returns in the 'new age'; it may be necessary to add that 'worship' here means, not adulation, but profound gratitude, awed wonder, the earnest of flawless joy and final fulfilment. This, in my submission, is the *point* of religion, what it proves in the end to be all about, for this is the object of the inarticulate desire that brings religion into being.

We now come to the regular objections to traditional theism made by process thinkers. The first of them will be discussed more fully later in connection with other writers, but the substance of the reply to it will be offered here. 'We are told by psychologists', our authors say, 'and we know from our experience that love in the fullest sense involves a sympathetic response to the loved one.

[1]*Op. cit.,* pp. 42-43.

Sympathy means feeling the feelings of the other...traditional theism said that God is completely impassive, and that there was no element of sympathy in his divine love for the creature'.[2] It is then pointed out that this was a difficulty for St Anselm and that St Thomas Aquinas had to conclude that God 'loves without passion' and that his love is purely 'outgoing' and not 'responsive'. So 'for Anselm and Thomas the analogy is with the father who has no feeling for his children, and hence does not feel their needs, but "loves" them in that he gives good things to them'.[3] The short answer to this, it seems to me, is that it is a mistake to assume that what is called for in ourselves must be called for also in God: that is to make God in our image. It is indeed the fact that, if we truly love someone who is in distress, we ourselves are distressed. But, strange though it may at first seem, it does not follow necessarily that it must be so for God. If we suppose that a friend of ours is not touched by our plight, we suspect that he does not really love us. If we hear him having an uproarious time in the house across the way while we are writhing in agony, we are tempted, understandably, to think him 'unfeeling'. But this is because love and 'feeling' are in fact *for us* bound up with one another in this way. When we complain that someone is 'unfeeling' it is not, or it ought not to be, because we *want* him to suffer as we are suffering but because, *unless* he so suffers, he doesn't love us. It is really his willingness to help us in our need that we value, his being at our disposal, his valuing of us which helps us to realize our *own* value, his generosity. Nothing of this is bound up intrinsically with 'feeling'. A Christian should know that God's attitude to us is one of unfailing generosity (despite apparent indication to the contrary). He gives us *ourselves* and, directly or indirectly, all that we value. He offers us *himself* to know and to love. What more can we ask of him? Does it make sense to suggest that he should suffer as and when his creatures do? He has joy, we

[2] P. 44.
[3] P. 45.

say. But must he have 'feelings'? To these questions I shall return in a later chapter.

There are three corollaries of the objection to a notion of love as purely creative. The first is that 'this implies that God loves some persons more than others', and St Thomas's words are quoted: 'No one thing would be better than another if God did not will greater good for one than for another'.[4] And this, we are told, 'is one of the central ways in which the notion of divine impassibility undercuts the biblical witness to the love of God'. The traditional view is that God gives different people different capacities. It is not, for instance, everyone's vocation to be a Carthusian monk: the proposal for a flat rate all round does not really make for general happiness. 'There is more in them', we can truly say of some people. But what others have it in them to do is, if they are willing, perfectly fulfilled in the end: their particular desires (which are not just the same as everyone else's) are completely satisfied. God loves us all, as we are, absolutely, that is, to the full. In the course of this discussion our authors have had occasion to remark that people are 'obviously not equal in regard to "the good things of life" (however these be defined) which they enjoy (especially in the context of traditional theism, where the majority are consigned to eternal torment)'. In other words, I take it, the God of traditional theism is thought to be responsible for everything in this world, including the sins of his creatures and their effects upon his providential ordering, and also responsible for the eternal torments of most of them. It is true that it was taken for granted for a long time, and not only by the less educated, that most people went to hell, and this is perhaps the most startling aberration in the history of Christian theology; but it was, of course, never part of the Church's official teaching. Nor is it part of that teaching that God 'consigns' people to hell. Reflective traditional Christians will be found to agree that God does not *punish*: since we are free, it is possible for

---

[4]P. 46. The reference is to the *Summa Theologiae*, Part I, question 20, art. 2.

someone to reject God absolutely, and in that case his[5] specifically human potential would come to nothing. What that condition would be like we do not know, but it is natural that Christians, for whom union with God is everything, should regard it, by *contrast*, as terrible in the extreme, even though we no longer talk about devils with pitchforks.

The second corollary is that the traditional notion of God's love 'has promoted a "love" which is devoid of genuine sensitivity to the deepest needs of the "loved ones" and hence the pejorative expression "do-gooder"'. It had never occurred to me that the mind of a 'do-gooder' might be working in terms of a misconceived theology, but the possibility cannot be ruled out.

The third corollary is that this traditional notion was bound up with 'the value-judgment that independence or absoluteness is unqualifiedly good, and that dependence or relativity in any sense derogates from perfection'.[6] But independence and absoluteness are not the whole truth about the God whom Christians worship: he is in no way dependent upon the world and his infinite perfection is changeless, but he is triune; that is, the one God is not *a* person but a society of super-persons, Father, Son, and Spirit, who are *interdependent*. This is a topic on which more, eventually, will be said.

One's suspicions that our authors confuse traditional theology with Calvinism is soon definitely confirmed: 'In traditional theological thought, all events were understood to be totally caused by God, so all events were "acts of God". However, most events were understood to be caused by God through the mediation of worldly or natural causes. God was the "primary cause" of these events, while the natural antecedents were called "secondary causes". However, a few events [miracles] were thought to be

---

[5]I have tried to avoid 'sexist language' in deference to female sensitivities, but in this particular instance I shall be forgiven, I hope, for not writing 'his or her'.

[6]P. 47.

caused directly by God, without the use of secondary causes'.[7] We are then told that 'there are two major problems with this notion'. First, 'it raises serious doubt that the creative activity of God can be understood as *love*, since it creates an enormous problem of evil by implying that *every* event in the world is *totally* caused by God, with or without the use of natural causes'. The second problem is that 'since the Renaissance and the Enlightenment, the belief has grown that there are no events which happen without natural causes'.[8] As for that, it must suffice to say here that, in the traditional view, all fresh being comes from God—it is a gift that adds to the activity of some part of the existing world—and that what we call 'laws of nature' are his ordering of the world in regular ways (a miracle is an exception to this regular ordering made in special circumstances). The first problem is in fact a mare's nest, since God's omnipotence has for its scope, according to the tradition, his gifts to the world but not our refusals of them. This must be examined at greater length.

The astonishing misconception that, as our authors put it in their Foreword,[9] 'God determines every detail of the world' in traditional theology seems to have been taken over by process thinkers from Whitehead's writings. In his popular *Adventures of Ideas,* for instance, we find this about the conclusions reached by 'the Christian theologians': 'The nature of God was exempted from all the metaphysical categories which applied to the individual things in this temporal world. . . . He stood in the same relation to the whole world as early Egyptian or Mesopotamian kings stood to their subject populations. . . . The worst of unqualified omnipotence is that it is accompanied by responsibility for every detail of every happening'.[10] After, in effect, repeating that, Cobb and Griffin add: 'Some traditional theologians, such as Thomas Aquinas, muted

[7]P. 49.
[8]P. 50.
[9]P. 9.
[10]*Op. cit.,* pp. 216-217.

this implication of their thought as much as possible (in order to protect the doctrine of human freedom). Others, such as Luther and Calvin, proclaimed the doctrine from the housetops. . . .'. If there is a 'doctrine of human freedom' for traditional theologians, as our authors here admit, then their complaint should be, not that human freedom was denied, but that the doctrine of divine omnipotence is inconsistent with it. (Calvinism, in rejecting human freedom, *opposes* the tradition.) However, they add: 'in either case, the doctrine [of Divine omnipotence, Calvinistically interpreted] followed logically from other doctrines which were affirmed'. It will be useful to notice how they make that out before undertaking a general defence of the traditional position:

> The notion that God knows the world, and that this knowledge is unchanging, suggests that God must in fact determine every detail of the world, lest something happen that was not immutably known. The doctrine that God is completely independent of the world implies that the divine knowledge cannot be dependent upon it, and this can only be if the world does nothing which was not totally determined by God. The doctrine of divine simplicity involves the assertion that all the divine attributes are identical; hence God's knowing the world is identical with God's causing it.[11]

God's knowledge of the changing world is itself unchanging because God knows, not in endless time, but in eternity, which is timeless. Our present, past, and future are all 'present' (timelessly) to him. He knows his gifts to ourselves and to our world in giving them (in this way 'God's knowing the world is identical with God's causing it'); it is true that he 'depends' on us for his knowledge of our refusals and their harmful effects, but this does not mean that we can *create* anything (sin has been called a 'decreation'), nor can we in any way impair him. The divine 'simplicity', properly understood, means that there is not in him that sort of complexity which calls for an explanation

---

[11]Cobb and Griffin, p. 52.

from outside it. Of the attributes in general it would be better to say that they involve one another rather than that they are identical.

The divine omnipotence, then, must not be interpreted, and has not been interpreted by mainstream Christianity, in such a way as to deny man's freedom to choose or reject God. We are doing one or the other, commonly without realizing it, whenever we make a moral choice or rather, perhaps, we are moving in the direction of doing one or the other (many contemporary thinkers consider that it is not until the moment of death that this choice is *fully* made). Dr E. L. Mascall has written of 'two Christian truths': 'first, that when a man acts in accordance with God's will God is not excluded from the act or reduced to the condition of a spectator but is the primary agent in it; secondly, that when a man tries to exclude God from the act and makes himself the primary agent, all that he manages to do is to introduce an element of sheer destruction and negation, an element which is not activity but rather deficiency . . .'. [12] When we are faced by alternative courses of action so that we have to ask ourselves 'what *ought* I to do?' and then realize *what* we ought to do, *we* can decide what is going to happen. We may fail to come up to scratch, and then we do something that is contrary to God's will, perhaps only *missing* the chance to do someone a service, perhaps doing some kind of more positive damage. God must enable us to perform all physical acts, just as he must continue to keep us in being, if we are to be choosers in a material world. But by refusing his offers and choosing another course *we* are responsible for the consequences. That, I believe, is the proper analysis of this famous difficulty. [13]

[12]*Nature and Supernature*, (Darton Longman and Todd, 1973), p. 81.

[13]On this see *Providence and Freedom*, (Burns & Oates, London, and Hawthorne Books, 1960) by Dom Mark Pontifex. Moral evil arises in the *turning away* from what God offers and so from God, with the result that the alternative attracting object exercises effective, undisputed influence. With this God has simply nothing to do; that is, it has nothing

Theologians have sometimes caused trouble, it must be admitted, by proposing that God 'permits' sin because he knows that all will come out best in the end that way, or by trying to make out that, somehow or other, everything happens according to God's will—if not his 'antecedent' will, then his 'consequent' one (for the sinner will not escape the consequences of his sin). There is no need, I think, to argue against such notions. When it is said that God *controls* his world, what should be meant is that he has a purpose for it that will not be defeated, the union of mankind with himself in Christ, the 'new heavens' and the 'new earth', not that all will infallibly achieve the goal set before them nor that all will go according to plan in the present life. So when Cobb and Griffin say that, 'The divine creative activity involves risk' and that 'since God is not in complete control of the events of the world, the occurrence of genuine evil is not incompatible with God's beneficence towards all his creatures', they are saying what has been normally said by traditional theologians. Yet these statements are part of their account of 'Whitehead's fundamentally new conception of divine creativity in the world'.[14] And they now declare that 'much of the tragedy in the course of human affairs can be attributed to the feeling that to control others, and the course of events, is to share in divinity'. Such a feeling is indeed horrific; I have been lucky enough never to have encountered in the flesh a clear case of it.

But there is certainly something in what follows: 'Although traditional theism said that God was essentially love, the divine love was subordinated to the divine power'. I must agree that 'the result of Jesus' message, life, and

to do with his 'omnipotence'. This view has seemed to me generally taken for granted in recent years, so it was disappointing to find in the first book review in the current issue (May 14, 1983) of the London *Tablet* the statement (made twice), by a well-known Dominican, that the problem of reconciling God's omnipotence with human free-will is 'unsolved'. I ought to add that Karl Rahner in *Theological Investigations* vol. 19, pp. 194-208, regards it as insoluble.

[14]P. 53.

death should have been to redefine divine power in terms of divine love', but when it is added baldly that 'this did not happen', I want to say rather that it did not always happen: our authors' next statement that power 'in the sense of controlling domination, remained the *essential* definition of deity' is contradicted by so much theological writing which insists that 'love' is the best 'pointer' to the strictly indescribable God. It is true that we in the West have been emerging only recently from a theological atmosphere heavily impregnated with a sort of legalism, but God's love has never been put formally in second place. It might be pointed out that liturgical prayers so often begin: 'Almighty and everliving God', and I should agree that in this there is a one-sided emphasis. (There are signs that it may be changed before very long.) But there is also to be borne in mind the fact that, at least for traditional Christians, the omnipotence of God, understood as I have urged that it has to be understood, calls for man's awe and amazement. Someone brought up in a secularized culture, for which 'God' has become almost meaningless, when he comes to believe in a creative power present and active at every place and at every moment in the world's history, will not find it at all uninteresting to address this power, in the first instance, as 'almighty and everliving God'. Perhaps all Christians need to be reminded of how stupendous is their belief in God, 'Creator of heaven and earth'. With the general contention of the passage under consideration that love, both human and divine, persuades and does not coerce, no traditional Christian should disagree.

Now we come to the charge that, for the tradition, 'God has been understood as Cosmic Moralist in the sense of being *primarily* concerned with the development of moral behaviour and attitudes in human beings. Negatively, this meant that the promotion of creaturely enjoyment was not God's first concern. In fact, in most Christian circles enjoyment has been understood as something that God at best tolerated...'.[15] The writers seem not to realize that

[15]P. 54.

the traditional principle of Christian morality is the love of God, with which love of one's neighbor is indissolubly bound up, and that its aim is the proper development not only of ourselves but of all with whom we come in contact in view of our common life in God, which begins here and is achieved hereafter. We are destined for joy. Enjoyment is frowned upon by the tradition only when its objects are, in the circumstances, harmful, although it must be admitted that 'the pleasure of sexual relations' came to be frowned upon by many Christians as though there were something wrong with it in itself. This deplorable attitude, encouraged by the prevalence of sexual greed and the damage done by unbridled sexual urges, has grown up in various human societies and is far from special to traditional Christian ones. Our authors, however, continue: 'This attitude toward sex is only the extreme example of the Church's traditional attitude towards enjoyment in general, which has been taken to be a reflection of God's attitude'. Here I cannot help feeling, not for the first time, that such statements must spring from an experience of Christianity largely confined to certain forms of Protestantism. The statement, with reference to 'the Christian Church', that 'moral goodness has primarily been understood negatively, that is, as involving the suppression of many of the natural forms of enjoyment'[16] is otherwise inexplicable. The passage which follows must be quoted at some length:

> This notion of God as Cosmic Moralist is not unrelated to the idea of God as Controlling Power. The problem of evil would too evidently disprove the existence of God, if God be understood not only as controlling all events, but also of willing the maximum enjoyment of his creatures. . . . Hence, the notion that God is competently in control of all things can be saved by saying that creaturely enjoyment is not a high priority. In fact, the sufferings of life, and even the inequities in this regard, can be regarded as divinely intended means to promote the desired moral and religious attitudes.

[16]P. 55.

If the problem of evil presented itself to traditional theologians in this light they would have argued that the sorrows of this life were somehow the necessary preliminary to the joys of the next. And what would these 'moral and religious attitudes' amount to? Just servility?

The remaining charges against the tradition are that it has encouraged submission to the *status quo* and that its concept of God 'is in many respects stereoscopically masculine', which latter charge proves to repeat previous objections summed up in the following remarkable sentence: 'God was conceived to be active, impassive, inflexible, impatient, and moralistic'.[17] The former charge is of more interest. It introduces us to Whitehead's idea of God as the great Adventurer: 'Besides the two senses already mentioned in which God's love is adventurous—that it takes risks and promotes adventure towards novelty in the world—there is a third sense...God's own life is an adventure, for the novel enjoyments which are promoted among the creatures are then the experiences providing the material for God's own enjoyment', but 'God will feel the discord as well as the beautiful experiences involved in the finite actualizations'.[18] How does Whitehead know all these things? And does this sort of talk about God seem to be in place? There are many professed agnostics who have (or who think they have) lost their childhood's faith but who would say: 'If there were a God, he would certainly not be like that'. For the Christian tradition, life is a journey, and the world has a history in which we have our parts to play; but it is not interested in novelty or even 'beautiful experiences' simply for their own sakes. If there is an objection to be faced about backing the *status quo*, it regards chiefly the alliance of throne and altar. This can be a very good thing, but it can also lead to very bad results. What understandably puts people off Christianity proves so often to flow in the end from the Church's becoming 'established', the gaining of temporal power. The blood of

[17]P. 61.
[18]Pp. 60-61.

the martyrs is the seed of the Church: the disappearance from her of merely conventional Christians may be expected perhaps to be equally, though less directly, productive.

To complete this account of process theology's most important positions, there are only two passages in our authors' fourth chapter ('A Theology of Nature') which need detain us. The first reads: 'Traditional theology has trouble explaining why there should be a world. The description of deity as *actus purus* meant that God had already actualized all possible values'.[19] This suggests that God had to actualize himself. But the point being made is that, since God is perfect for traditional theology, he could have no reason for creating an imperfect world. For process theology, we are now reminded, 'possible values all subsist in God...as merely *possible* values, not as actualized.... They are possible values for finite realization'. In other words, God knows that it is possible for *us* to actualize them if he encourages us to do so, and only in that way can they become actual values for *him*. I find it puzzling that this metaphysical hypothesis should have been welcomed by so many intelligent persons. The point at issue, however, is whether, for the tradition, there was any point in God's actualizing the world. Without it, all was well. Would he not have done better to leave well alone? Indeed, if reality was already complete in him, how *could* he have done anything about it? The mistake here is to suppose that there is something called 'reality', actualized or unactualized, which is shared by God with ourselves. For traditional theology (or rather for traditional philosophy, for this is not all *defined* doctrine), the transcendence of God means that there is nothing strictly in common between him and ourselves. We can 'imitate' him, but he is always 'beyond' anything that our concepts can contain. If it is urged that he must have such of our values as are conceivable, freed from limitations (love in particular), one must reply that they are such pale shadows of his that they

[19]P. 63.

cannot be added up along with his to form a whole. But that is not to say that they were not worth creating—for the sake of his creatures themselves, not for God's. Process thinkers seem unable to conceive of a super-agent with an activity which is purely 'outgoing' in the sense that *he* gets nothing out of it.

In the second passage we discover a change of front: 'Many theologians and philosophers of religion have proposed a "free-will defence" of God's goodness. The central claim is that moral evil (which as an evil intention is itself evil and in its consequences is the cause of most of the suffering in our world) occurs, even though God is all-good and all-powerful, because God out of his goodness decided to give freedom to human beings'.[20] It cannot be supposed that there is anything new about what has come to be called the 'free-will defence' so far as described in this passage. So the original charge that, for traditional theology, 'God determines every detail of the world' seems now to have been tacitly dropped. Our authors, however, have more to say: 'But there is a serious objection to this theodicy: it takes the form of doubt that freedom is really such an inherently great thing that it is worth running the risk of having creatures such as Hitler'. They conclude that this 'reduces to the question as to whether the positive values enjoyed by the higher forms of actuality are worth the risk of the negative values—the sufferings'.[21] (Here again we have to remember that these higher forms of 'actuality' are not thought of as surviving death.) And their answer to the question takes the form of putting these further questions: 'Should we risk suffering, in order to have a shot at intense enjoyment? Or should we sacrifice intensity, in order to minimize possible grief?', with a reminder that 'the divine reality . . . is an Adventurer, choosing the former mode . . .'. Whitehead's God does not know what is coming to him. 'The eternal God, who is supposed to know everything timelessly', so an objector might break

20P. 74.
21P. 75.

in here, 'knows what Hitler is up to, so why did he create him?' I should reply that God's knowing everything time-lessly means that he just *sees* everything that happens, and that he cannot *see* Hitler's goings on unless Hitler is going to be created. In that sense, God runs a risk, but not in the sense that he is ever surprised. A final reflection on all this may already be obvious: traditional theology, with its very different understanding of the divine, has another way of dealing with the question: why did God give us freedom? But we shall be considering this in due course.

At this half-way point in the book which has engaged us for so long, Cobb and Griffin turn to questions of Christian belief and practice which will be discussed later, so far as necessary, in connection with other writers. But there is one other sentence which deserves quotation because it points so directly to the heart of my disagree-ments with them: 'God is impoverished when the rich complexity of the biosphere is reduced'.[22] And I should like to give one more instance, in conclusion, of the many significant passages with which everyone should be able to agree:

> In its openness to the creative love of God, the self receives new possibilites for its own existence that point it away from itself towards wider horizons of interest. Through its open-ness to the responsive love of God, it receives assurance of its acceptance in spite of its sin, is freed from preoccupation with itself, and is enabled to turn to others with a disinterested concern for their welfare.[23]

I must now turn to a charge against the tradition which has not yet been mentioned. Belief in 'subjective' (per-sonal) immortality is suspected in some quarters of being immoral. Writing about this belief and a belief in a 'wholly external scheme of supernatural rewards and punish-ments', Schubert M. Ogden wrote, twenty years ago:

[22]P. 152.
[23]P. 95. God's love, I want to say, can be 'responsive' without *adding* anything to him, as our authors suppose. Apart from that, there is clearly common ground in this passage.

'Both of these beliefs I regard as highly questionable, and that in large part because of what I can only describe as their moral crudity. I suspect not only that one can be moral without them, but that it is hard to be moral on any other terms'.[24] Christians believe in God's love for us and that he will unite us with him when we die if we do not refuse him. Ogden has in mind, presumably, the picture of an arbitrary tyrant who likes to keep people cringing before him and tortures them everlastingly for disobedience. In his own view, 'it is as easy to conceive God as the eminent *effect* of all things as to think of him as their eminent *cause*' and so 'in making each of us the object of his boundless love, God accepts us all into his own everlasting life and thereby overcomes both our death and our sin'.[25] *We* disappear, apparently, in the process; we give ourselves to God in that sense. If we expect anything just for ourselves, then we are not 'serving' God, for 'it is *God himself* who is the only final end'.[26] Ogden assumes that our achievements must be thrown to waste unless they add to God's happiness and that nothing but this should be our aim: 'What profit could it be for us to go on and on living—even to eternity—if the net result of all our having lived were simply nothing; if our successive presents in no way added up to a cumulative accomplishment such as no creature is able to provide either for himself or for his fellows?'[27] I think this vision of things myopic, but it cannot be denied that there is a nobility about it, just as there is in the vision of morality for the sake of morality in the Kantian tradition and in the writings of Iris Murdoch.

But, as we read on, we find to our surprise that Ogden has been putting up a case to which he does not commit himself. At first, indeed, in the discussion of eschatology which follows he seems to go into reverse: 'What we are, and so what we shall be forever in the final judgment of

[24]*The Reality of God*, (S.C.M. Press), p. 36.
[25]*Op. cit.*, p. 223.
[26]P. 221.
[27]P. 225.

God's love, is just what we decide in the present through our responsible freedom. If we choose to open ourselves to God in faith and in love for him and all those whom he loves, then this is who we are, and this is who we will be known to be in God's righteous judgment. If, on the other hand, we shut ourselves off from God and our fellows ...then this, too, is who we are and who God, in consequence, will judge us to be even to the farthest reaches of eternity.... The very meaning of "hell" is to be bound to God forever without the faith in his love which is the peace that passes understanding'.[28] It is difficult, after that, not to think that the inhabitants of hell are, in Ogden's view, more than just the objects of God's memory. But on the next page we read: 'At the risk of anti-climax, I am constrained to add that the interpretation of the promise of faith presented here leaves completely open the question whether we somehow manage to survive death and continue to exist as experiencing subjects as is claimed by conventional theories of immortality'.

Dr Norman Pittenger, a close friend of Charles Hartshorne, tells us that the latter 'is himself inclined to reject personal immortality on the ground that to wish for it is to indulge in a kind of selfishness which refuses to accept and rejoice in any accomplishment of goodness or truth or beauty unless "I" can have a personal share in its triumph'.[29] Hartshorne, in a recently published book, has remarked that in it 'the view is favored that only the primordial being can be everlasting'.[30] I find his objection as reported by Pittenger obscure, but I suppose it must be the same as Ogden's. That morality consists in aiming at the Good without thought for one's personal advantage is obviously the case when there is a *choice* between the Good and one's personal advantage. But there can be no selfishness in accepting a gift which, we believe, God offers. Pittenger

---

[28]P. 227-228.

[29]*Process Thought and Christian Faith*, (Nisbet, Welwyn, 1968), p. 80.

[30]*Creative Synthesis and Philosophic Method*, (University of America Press, 1983), p. 121.

suggests that 'since the basic drive through the entire created order is unselfish action towards further good', Hartshorne regards the desire for immortality as 'in flat contradiction to the purpose of creation'; this seems to imply a myth of Progress in which everything happens for the sake of something else indefinitely. When Christians say that persons have value in themselves, what they mean is that God gives them value by giving them the capacity for union with him. And they do not love God *because* he will unite them with himself but because they see in him the source of all value. Love is outgoing, ecstatic, and they 'go out' to him because he is who he is. That they should find their fulfilment in him cannot then be objectionable.

'It seems to me', Pittenger continues (he is in general agreement with process thought), 'that Hartshorne has here permitted his justified dislike of certain popular ways of envisaging the possibility of immortality to dominate his thinking. The sort of approach which he condemns is indeed self-centred to an unfortunate degree...'. Do these popular notions, then, envisage immortality as the gift of goods for private consumption like innumerable cases of champagne? Pittenger then suggests a more plausible approach to the topic: 'Precisely because God is love and precisely because the achievement of greater good, especially through the activity of such personalized occasions as man may be said to be, is itself a good, may not the achieved good include the agency *by which it was achieved?* May not the satisfaction of the subjective aim include as a necessary consequence some sort of persistence of the creaturely agent, and cannot this persistence itself enhance the ongoing process?' And he refers to 'a joy that is shared "in widest commonalty" in and with God'. But this is not enough. If the traditional belief in personal immortality is to make good sense, it must be made clear that the *worship* of God is basic to it. If we are to talk about an 'ongoing process', it is not the piling up of goods which are the combined product of God and 'such personalized occasions as man may be said to be' but the ever-deepening contemplation of God's inexhaustible perfection which is best 'pointed to' by calling it beauty.

Whitehead, notoriously, had no interest in our topic. Dr E. L. Mascall has pointed out that 'his final attitude to God is not one of adoration so much as of sympathy';[31] it is not, he suggests, without significance that the famous description of God as 'the great companion—the fellow-sufferer who understands'—is the conclusion of *Process and Reality*. But it would be an exaggeration to say that Whitehead's work is a cosmology spiced by late-Victorian religiosity, for from time to time it strikes a deeper note. This is true also of his successors. The presence of God to the human mind is the source of our finest aspirations, and these can be rising to the surface even when they take misguided forms in which they seem to call for our annihilation rather than our fulfilment. There is nothing individualistic about personal union with God. Process thinkers are clearly right in emphasizing interrelatedness. But interrelatedness is important because it enhances the value of distinct persons. And the value of persons is not properly appreciated without that attention to God's presence in us which is prayer. It is the concentration of process thinkers upon outward activity, getting things done, pushing ahead with the world's business, which makes them seem sometimes to be just a type of secular humanists. They show up the abuses of Christian faith, but they misconstrue it.

[31]*He Who Is*, (Darton Longman and Todd, 1966), p. 157.

III
The Importance of Professor Hartshorne

There is one charge against the tradition which was saved for this chapter because it is specially associated with the veteran philosopher Charles E. Hartshorne, the acknowledged leader among process thinkers in our time. The charge to which I refer seems to me justified. It bears, I shall suggest, not on a traditional Christian doctrine but on the way in which the doctrine, that of God's freedom in creating, has been regularly interpreted, namely as the freedom to choose not only what is to be created but whether there is to be creation at all. Hartshorne makes his point in the briefest and most effective form in his Aquinas Lecture delivered at Marquette University in 1976: 'Whatever God is, that he could not fail to be: hence if God is the decider who wills "Let there be such and such a world", he could not have failed to be that very decider'.[1] In other words, the traditional doctrine of God's immutability is incompatible with the traditional doctrine of his freedom in creating, understood as freedom to *choose* whether or what to create, because his act of creating is identified with his 'nature', that is, with himself. That seems to me unanswerable; I have proposed that this doctrine should be interpreted as referring not to freedom of *choice* but to freedom from restraint of any kind and that no question of God's *not* creating should arise. It does not follow that his creatures are necessary in the sense of being independent of him or that he needs to create in the

[1] *Aquinas to Whitehead: Seven Centuries of Metaphysics of Religion*, (Marquette University Publications, Milwaukee), p. 19.

sense of gaining something for himself by his creating.[2] Fr Norris Clarke is clearly thinking along much the same lines when, after speaking of the doctrine of the Trinity ('it illumines how God's own inner life is already rich in infinite self-expression'), he continues: 'It is then quite freely— although one might well say *inevitably*, according to the natural "logic" of love—without any need or desire for further self-enrichment, but purely out of the joy of giving that the divine love can pour over to share itself with creatures'.[3] But all this needs to be explained and defended at some length.

The Thomist position is thus stated by Fr F. C. Copleston: 'On the one hand Aquinas was convinced that as a personal and perfectly self-luminous being God must have chosen intelligently out of the infinite realm of possibility the finite things which he has created. He was not compelled by his nature to create or to create this or that possible world'.[4] Copleston is referring to the well-known doctrine that God sees himself as 'imitable' in innumerable different ways: there are innumerable possible worlds which could 'reflect' his perfection in the created order, each in its own special way. God finds himself faced with these innumerable possibilities waiting to be realized. He need not realize any of them. And it is commonly added, when this doctrine is expounded, that no 'possible world' chosen by God could be the *best* possible world, because any world, being finite, could always be 'better' than it is—there could always be, so to speak, 'more to it'. It seems to me that this account of divine creation is implausible: God's choice of a world seems purely arbitrary, and it seems improper for him to be faced with a choice at all. The unchanging God, I want to say, simply does 'his thing'. There seems to be no cogent reason why we should not say that our world is simply his one world, the world destined to produce the supreme

---

[2]The first book of mine in which this thesis appeared was *An Essay in Christian Philosophy*, (Longmans, 1954), pp. 93-102. So far as I know, it has not been controverted.

[3]*Op. cit.*, p. 88. I am not happy with this language of 'sharing'.

[4]*Aquinas*, (Penguin Books), p. 144, (p. 139 as originally printed).

instance of created goodness, the uniquely sinless one, the unrepeatable expression in human terms of the divine Word, Jesus Christ, the new Adam, head of a renewed race. Obviously a great deal has gone wrong with the world. According to the tradition, this is the result of sin, angelic as well as human.

It has not escaped the notice of the more reflective traditional theologians that possible worlds cannot be said to *exist*—this is only a picturesque way, they tell us, of saying that God is completely free in creating (some contemporary philosophers say that they do exist but are not 'actual', a position which I find incomprehensible). And they are ready to allow that freedom and necessity, when the limitations which attach to them in ourselves are removed, converge in God. To refer to God as 'necessary' being is to say that he cannot not be; he is independent, free in that sense, wholly without constraint in being himself. To say that he simply *is* is to say that everything else is what it is because he made it so. But he is best 'pointed to' as the Source of being. His creating is both absolutely free and absolutely necessary. Freedom to choose is the limited freedom of one in a particular situation. God is the reason why there are any situations. Although he is strictly indescribable, our knowledge of him is knowledge not of a blank but of a richness: 'absolute value' is the 'pointing' phrase in this connection. To put this in context I must now repeat myself. In knowing God as relating personally to us, we know that there are in him those values which are found in created persons and are conceivable in an unlimited form. This we can know because we can be in actual contact, however obscure, with the ultimate value of love, that is, supergenerosity, involving consciousness and creative power. Freedom and necessity, then, are not the only values that converge at infinity.

Thomists who disapprove of the proposal that God does not choose to create but just creates may refer to Vatican I's condemnation of the view that he creates by necessity of 'nature'. What the condemnation was aimed at was clearly the danger of suggesting some form of 'emanationism' by using the language of 'necessity'. Such language might imply that God *gave* something of himself in a literal sense in creating his world, or that the world added something to him so that he and the world could be thought of as forming together somehow a single whole. So it was the threat of pantheism that such condemnations envisaged, and it should be clear that no such threat lurks behind my proposal: God's creating can be called 'necessary' only in the same sense as that in which it can be called 'free', a sense in which all that is positive in our usual understanding of these notions is retained and all that is negative is excluded. But the best way of putting it, I suggest, is to say that we have no business to ask questions about what God could have done or might have done. The language about God's doings which is the least open to misconstruction uses its verbs in the present indicative—with the warning that in reality *time* does not come into it at all.

In the past Thomists have argued that, because God and the world cannot be added up, therefore the existence of the world makes no difference to him, which is true in the sense that there has been no time for him before it was created (it has 'always' been there) but which they asserted with the meaning that he would be just the same whether he created it or not. That is an excuse for the charge that the Thomist God has no interest in the world, although such a conception would be inconsistent with so much else in the Thomist system. Hartshorne's rebuttal stands: if God had not made the decision to create, he would not be the sort of agent that we know him to be. And it may be further objected against the Thomists, those of the past at least, that talk about God's leaving a capacity to create unactualized is unacceptable. To say that God's power is limitless and that he cannot have used it all up is to suppose that power is something that he *has*, waiting to be drawn upon. But all that we are entitled to say is that God acts in an unrestricted way. The notion of unrealized potentialities in God, far from exalting him, seems to imply change and limitations. Does it make sense to suggest that he could have acted less generously or more generously than he has done?

To consider Hartshorne's Aquinas Lecture in some detail will show his other objections to 'traditional theology' and at the same time his own rival positions so far as they may claim to concern us. The first point of dispute is 'an example of seemingly self-evident truth which for two thousand years escaped critical examination'.[5] He finds this in Plato's *Republic* where 'deity is defined as perfect, meaning possessed of a value so great that no increase or improvement would be conceivable, and no decrease either, since the possibility of such corruption would be a defect'.[6] Aristotle took over this doctrine and concluded that such a being 'can have no unactualized potentiality in its reality; whatever it could be, it is'.[7] Hartshorne continues his exposition as follows:

> Any relations between deity and contingent events in the world (relations which might have been otherwise, since the events might have been otherwise) will qualify the events, not deity.... Just this is what Aquinas asserts when he says that relations between God and the world are relations for the world but not for God.... But Aristotle deduces a momentous corollary: since to know something is to be related to it...God cannot know contingent and changeable things.

We have encountered this objection in principle before. Aquinas is concerned to show that God is not changed by his knowledge of the world. His knowledge of it does not change because he knows it timelessly. But the events in the world would not be what they are if human beings had made choices other than those which in fact they made. So God seems to *depend* on them for his knowledge. God, however, *enables* their physical acts whether they accept or refuse his offers of good. All fresh being in the world

---

[5]*Op. cit.,* p. 4.

[6]Pp. 4-5.

[7]Pp. 6-7. The argument which follows is often repeated by Hartshorne's disciples, e.g., Ogden, *The Reality of God,* p. 133

depends on him for its existence and he knows it as such. For the refusal of his offers his creatures are wholly responsible, and he knows these refusals for what they are, negations which have nothing to do with him. Aquinas says that, 'There are some good things which can be corrupted by evil things, and so God would not know good things completely unless he also knew evil ones'.[8] I cannot claim his agreement for all that I am saying here, but it will be clear from this that his view cannot be adequately summed up by Hartshorne's account of it:[9] 'God is the cause of all things, and in knowledge of a cause its effects are known; hence in merely knowing himself God must know whatever things he could produce and needs no further relation to the things'. This, Hartshorne says here, inverts 'the sole ontological epistemic relation, which is the one actualized in the knowing rather than in the known' (in other words, the true account is that the knower, not the known, is affected when there is knowledge). It is true that Aquinas, by constantly asserting that God knows the world 'through his essence' (to avoid a specification of God's intellect by created things), can seem to imply that his knowledge does not bear on *them* but only on his unrealized 'idea' of them. Perhaps we may put what he was driving at in a more acceptable way by saying that God sees his world and everything that happens in it in virtue of his creative power, which is not to be thought of as other than his love and which unchangingly offers the world what is best in all the changing circumstances for which our own refusals are largely responsible. It must be granted that there is a *complexity* in God's knowledge which traditional thought has been generally unwilling to admit. Hartshorne, in all this, has been working up to his own answer to the question, that God knows the world and changes on one 'side' of him: 'God may have accidents as well as essence, and with respect to the latter, but not to the former, he may be asymmetrically independent of the actual world'.[10]

[8]*Summa Theologiae*, I, question XIV, art. X (corp.).
[9]*Op. cit.*, pp. 10-11.
[10]P. 12.

So after concluding that, if God is necessary, there might seem to be only a choice between saying that everything else is also necessary and saying that God does not know everything, Hartshorne writes, 'A third possibility remains: admit contingency and change in the deity as well as in the world'.[11] He goes on to say, 'It was the little noticed heretical Christian sect of the Socinians who dared to take this step.... The Socinians took human freedom seriously, interpreting this to mean that human decisions, so far as free, cannot be known in advance, since in advance they do not exist to be known'. Then, referring to the view that these decisions 'are known not in advance but eternally', he remarks, 'The idea of events spread out for contemplation in a finished series, some future to us, is a form of the "spatializing of time"', indicted (he adds) by Bergson. This is the way in which we try to *imagine* God's timeless knowledge of time, but an *apprehension* of God shows that imagination is not here in place: we know that God is unimaginable because he is apprehended as 'beyond' time. Hartshorne, however, continues as follows:

> If God acquires new knowledge as new things are there to be known, the eternity of God cannot mean his immutability. 'God is eternal', the Socinians said, 'in that he cannot not exist'. This implies that the divine essence (what makes God God and not a mere creature) is necessarily actualized somehow, that is, in some states of knowledge that are omniscient in the sense defined, yet with contingent aspects and with significant increments as reality itself acquires new items. There is in this knowledge no loss but only gain.[12]

Thus God does not know what is going to happen tomorrow until tomorrow comes. Like human beings, he 'can change in some respects without changing in every respect.... We can appeal to the Aristotelian principle that the abstract is real in the concrete, for the essence or ultimate purpose is abstract and the specific aims are con-

[11]P. 13.
[12]P. 14.

crete'.[13] In a recent issue of *Religious Studies*[14] Mr. J. L. Tomkinson's article, 'Divine Simplicity and Atemporality', refers to the increasingly frequent reductions of God's timelessness to temporal duration without beginning or end, pointing out that, according to traditional doctrine, God's eternity is not 'the mere absence or irrelevance of time but rather a mode of existence less limiting than the temporal', and he suggests plausibly that these reductions are due rather to the *Zeitgeist* than to philosophical considerations. It has seemed to many minds that existence in time is a limitation which reveals to us our dependence on the Unlimited. For existence to be confined to this present evanescent form of it, a constant state of coming to be and passing away, seems impossible. The truth of the matter, I suggest, is that we should not recognize our impermanence as a problem unless we became aware, however dimly, that it is supported by ultimate changelessness. This is to come into collision with process thinkers in the most direct way. For them, becoming, change, is the ultimate reality; but it has been characteristic of religious thinkers that change is for them unintelligible unless it is relative to the Absolute, and the proposal of process thinkers that God should be relativized on one 'side' of him has been thus ruled out by them.

A discussion between process thinkers and traditional ones on this issue today could therefore go on indefinitely because the disputants have different starting points. For process thinkers, it is a mark of a sound metaphysical theory that it should be able to offer an account of God which fits in with our experience of ourselves; there are 'metaphysical principles' (in particular, that of creativity) which must apply to all realities, God included. For traditional thinkers, the first thing to be said about God is that he is *other* than ourselves, totally different in the sense that he lives on another 'plane', to which it is added that we stand to him nevertheless in a unique relationship which

[13]P. 23.
[14]Vol. 18, no. 2.

makes communion with him possible. Here is a claim to a fundamental experience, capable of becoming a matter of *certainty*, so that we cannot get behind it to find some criterion of truth with which to test it. What is experienced is totally mysterious; that is, we are aware that we cannot comprehend it, get our minds *round* it, but we know that it is there and that it is 'beyond' anything that our minds can get round. To speak of God's 'timelessness' is to speak of his freedom from temporal limitations, but we have no understanding of timelessness. We know that it means something to say that it is somehow inclusive of timefulness and superior to it and that this inclusiveness is to be taken in a non-spatial sense. But we can say that we have some inkling of a state of affairs which is non-spatial: there is a sense in which all experience is non-spatial, despite the current prejudice against any sort of 'dualism' in the human make-up. And we may even have an intimation of timelessness when we are, as we say, 'absorbed', seeming to be for once perfectly at peace, fixed, but yet 'more vividly alive than we otherwise know how to be'.[15] No reader of the later books of St Augustine's *Confessions* could be in doubt that the writer's references to timelessness are based not merely on an acceptance of Christian doctrine or on mere speculation but on an awareness which has somehow convinced him that the idea is verified. The note of rising excitement when this topic occurs (in 'the vision of Ostia', for instance) is unmistakable. It would be possible to say the same, in principle, of so many Christian mystics before and after Augustine.

To all this it may be replied that there is no limit to the extent to which human beings can deceive themselves (which is perhaps true, but in some cases seems hardly

[15]Harold Osborne, *Aesthetics and Criticism,* p. 229. This feature of aesthetic experience has been discussed by religious philosophers who claim that it can persist when the aesthetic object which provoked it is no longer being contemplated but has given place to what is completely indescribable. In other words, I suppose, it is a beginning of religious experience that may not become explicit for those who are not sufficiently prepared for it.

relevant) and that the notion of timelessness is incoherent. To say that God sees everything in a timeless present is incoherent, it has been claimed, because the future does not yet exist. Nor can God know what I know as 'now', part of a time-series, if he is himself 'outside' that series. And if his view of time is as different from ours as traditional theology would have it, then our view of it must be illusory. To take the last point first, we must admit or rather maintain that time taken as an isolated object of thought does seem unintelligible and has been regarded by some philosophers as therefore illusory. A sheer 'becoming' is unthinkable. So we are brought back to the ultimate point of dispute with process thinkers. But it may be added that the notion of time's ticking on everlastingly, as it does for their God, has something specially repugnant about it. A perfection which is not the result of a cessation of activity but is a super-activity in which our values of movement and of rest converge, transmuted, at infinity would seem to be the only alternative. The knowledge and love of the blessed, I have already suggested, must be in a mysterious sense processive because the Absolute is inexhaustible. But it is knowledge of the unchangeable, terminal knowledge. The other objections to timelessness mentioned above are based on the supposition that God's eternal *now* is to be taken in a literal sense. But God has no present in the sense of a moment of time. He sees what is for us past, present, and future in their relationships of before and after; he sees all that is the case, but he does not experience that limitation to a moment of time which is a mark of our finiteness. He knows 'now' that I am having this experience in the sense that it is *true* now that I am having it. All our verbs are tensed and we can speak of God without misleading only if we make clear that time-references must all be thought away. There is a sense in which Hartshorne's God is not mysterious *enough*. The rest of his lecture (largely concerned with the history of philosophy) will provide some further evidence to that effect.

'The whole point of contingency', he writes, 'lies here, that actualization, decision, is always exclusive of positive values'.[16] This is the principle of creativity; all events are brought about by a self-creative decision, even at the inorganic level. The contention is developed as follows:

> Even God must make contingent decisions to create a world: he must rule out *good* alternatives. Even he cannot have the values of all possible worlds, all fully actualized. According to Whitehead, this is the rationale for becoming, that no actuality can leave nothing further to seek. Divine potentiality for value is absolutely infinite, but not even divine actuality can ever exhaust this potentiality.

God, then, requires a world for the fresh values which it provides, a value which can be added to indefinitely. 'Hence', Hartshorne continues, after a reference to the doctrine of 'unincreasable perfection', 'process philosophy revises the definition of divine excellence.... God is ideally good and great, not by being an absolute and unincreasable maximum of value, but by being *unsurpassable by another* than himself...only God can surpass God, but this he perpetually does by absorbing the riches of creation into himself'.[17]

In another passage Hartshorne declares: 'We are influenced by God because we intuit God' (this being presumably the same as being 'lured' by God, as Whitehead put it, to choose the good). The passage continues:

> In process philosophy we, or the created minds, influence God for the same reason, that is, God intuits or, in Whitehead's phrase, 'prehends' them. The single principle of prehending, which is but an aspect of 'creativity' or experience, as, in principle and always, partly active or self-created, utilizing previous events as materials for fresh syntheses, the syntheses themselves furnishing new such materials and so on for ever—this principle expresses not only how the world hangs together, but also how it depends upon and yet also influences God.[18]

To a traditional Christian who recognizes God as the One,

[16]*Op. cit.*, p. 32.
[17]P. 33.
[18]P. 41.

incomparable, this can seem only a theory which might have the merits of economy and simplicity for a certain kind of philosopher but is obviously ruled out for a theologian. Hartshorne comments: 'No more magnificent metaphysical generalization has ever been made'. He goes on to say: 'Our final and inclusive end is to contribute to the divine life'. This refers to the view that our personal consciousness ceases with death, which has been discussed already in connection with Schubert Ogden, once Hartshorne's pupil. It is worth returning to this because of the passage which now follows:

> If this view seems to make God lacking in generosity, I suggest that the all-knowing and all-loving cannot give happiness to others without fully participating in and possessing this happiness just because it is realized by others. For such is love at its fullest, joy in the joy, and sorrow in the sorrow, of others. The injunction, 'seek to further a good beyond your own', applies to creatures that die and are more or less incapable of appreciating the benefits that they may bestow upon others. The imperishable and all-appreciating Eminent Being, however, can act for the good of all without transcending his own good as the inclusive goal. [19]

Hartshorne seems to be dealing with a possible objection and saying that God cannot help enjoying himself the happiness which he gives to others. But no one could complain of that state of affairs if it did not come to an end, so far as we are concerned, at our deaths. The complaint which would be pertinent is that God, in this account, is *incapable* of bringing us through death to life. As we saw in the last chapter, Hartshorne has expressed elsewhere the view in this connection that 'only the primordial being can be everlasting'. I shall be returning later to the topic of God's sorrows, but it may be remarked here that if 'we are contributors to the ever-growing divine treasury of values', as Hartshorne also says in the paragraph quoted above, his sorrows too must continue to pile up for ever.

[19]Pp. 43-44.

The next passage which demands notice underlines the ultimate question:

> The objection to the notion of creative causation, meaning that which produces a net increase in reality, was that the cause 'cannot give what it lacks'! As though temporal genesis were a mere passing out, or passing on, of something already real! Rather it is growth, passage from less to more, in short, creation. The effect is not 'given', it does not 'come from' some antecedent haven, it becomes . . . and this idea is ultimate. [20]

Certainly it is absurd to talk as though no genuine novelty appeared in the world. The theme, to which I have already referred, that all appearance of fresh being is due to God's creative power, is a traditional one (which is not to say that it has always been properly grasped by traditional thinkers). God uses his creatures, as soon as there are any, as instruments for his further creating ('as soon' must not be taken to mean that there was any *time* when creation had not happened). Our evidence for this, I have proposed, is basically our awareness that we are ourselves wholly dependent on him for our existence. This relation of total dependence is mysterious in the highest degree, as we should expect it to be. Anyone who says that the appearance of fresh being is just a fact for which no explanation can or need be found cannot be proved wrong but may be encouraged to take deeper soundings. Is there any solid reason to support a third proposal that creativity is the joint property of an everlasting being and ourselves?

Let us, then, take a last look at Hartshorne's position as shown in a passage which is, in effect, the conclusion of his Aquinas Lecture. Here he refers, apparently with complete approval, to the famous passage in which Whitehead summed up his own view about God's two 'sides': 'One side of God's nature is said to be "infinite, free, complete, primordial, eternal, actually deficient, and unconscious". The other side is "determined, incomplete, consequent, everlasting [meaning incorruptible, all changes being gain, not loss], fully actual, and conscious"...the consequent nature "originates with physical experience derived from the finite world and then acquires integration with the primordial side...". Infinity in the absolute sense is a conceptual entity concerned with possibilities as such, not a possible actuality'.[21] As Fr Norris Clarke remarks, 'nothing seems to be said of any *intrinsic* infinite fullness of perfection within God's own being in itself'. He goes on to say: 'It seems, then, that the entire satisfaction and conscious fulfilment of God is an *extroverted* one, absorbed entirely in guiding the world towards intelligibility and value and in treasuring up within himself the values actually achieved by it'.[22] I can only say that the picture seems to me unconvincing.[23]

[21]Pp. 50-51.

[22]*Op. cit.*, p. 87-88.

[23]Detailed and penetrating criticisms of Hartshorne's position will be found in Professor Robert Neville's *Creativity and God*, (The Seabury Press, New York, 1980). He has considerable sympathy with Hartshorne. I find his own account of God's relation to the world obscure, but it seems possible to retail one of his arguments in a short space by stringing together its main items. 'Let us assume', he writes, 'the process commitment to events and agree with the claim that an enduring individual is an event-sequence.... The event-sequence of a human being repeatedly exhibits the human arrangement of bodily parts ...perhaps one's dominantly mental events are one's own not so much because they repeat a pattern intrinsically, but rather because they feel themselves always to be taking place in the environment of one's body.... The feeling that all one's thoughts are *possessed by oneself* is not the only kind of continuity, however. Our experience seems committed to moral continuity. That is, one is obligated to keep promises, even if one has forgotten them.... One conceives oneself as having a unique life, a career, with problems of life style and leading a meaningful life. These conceptions do not make much sense unless one's integral continuity is more than the embodiment of all one's thoughts in the same body' (pp. 54-55).

Neville then proposes that an event-sequence of that kind should be granted 'essential data' ('factors determining the subjective form of the event') and points out that Hartshorne would be unwilling to grant this on the ground that human beings may be 'biased in fact by the implications of a surreptitious substance ontology'. For, according to Hartshorne, 'we should be open to the Hindu experience that continuity,

This chapter will be concluded with a discussion of a passage in which the Regius Professor of Divinity at Oxford, Maurice Wiles, regards the relation of God to the world as presenting an unsolved problem for any form of theism. It puts into a wider context the question of God's immutability discussed at the beginning of the chapter, and it may show that the Christian tradition has more work to do on the issue thus presented:

> Perhaps one of the most important distinctions between the Western and the Eastern theological traditions is to be found in the different point at which each has chosen to locate the crux of incoherence in relating God to the world. The West places it between God and the world. God is pure actuality; in him is no potency, nothing more waiting to be realized; complete in himself, he is in need of nothing for his own

when pressed, turns out to be the union of all in the world soul' or perhaps to the view of some Buddhists that 'continuity is a mere appearance covering a mere multiplicity of flashes of reality'. Neville comments: 'One of the greatest virtues Hartshorne sees in event-pluralism is that it does away with the metaphysical underpinning of ego-centrism and the self-interest theory of motivation.... Refutation of ego-centrism and self-interest by denying the self, however, seems extreme surgery' (pp. 56-57).

Some readers may be encouraged to tackle the whole chapter on Hartshorne in which Neville questions, among other things, his conception of the abstract and the concrete as two poles, the latter containing the former ('the truth of the matter may well be that something abstract merely is *known* because *an instance* of it is discovered in something concrete'), his conception of God's abstract nature as consisting in 'the a priori metaphysical conditions that would have to be exhibited in any possible world' (Neville argues that this is incompatible with Hartshorne's view that God is a society of 'occasions' which go on happening forever) and his view of the 'perishing' of Whitehead's 'actual occasions' as merely the fact that, when an occasion is said to 'perish', it becomes an object for further subjects (Neville points out that it 'has lost its *subjective feeling of being in process'*—Hartshorne here dodges the fact of evil). In the earlier chapters of his book Neville criticizes very effectively process thinkers' distinguishing of creativity from God, and he argues that Whitehead's idea of God as a single actual entity would make it impossible for him to prehend, or to be prehended by, a worldly 'occasion' at any finite time.

self-fulfilment. How, then, is it that he creates? Can his relation to his creatures be a real relation to himself? Can he give himself to his creation, or is the 'created grace' that he bestows something supernatural but less than himself?... The Eastern tradition is different. The religious ideal of divinization will allow of no such qualifications in the account of God's self-giving to man in grace. The point of incoherence is pushed back into the being of God himself. The point of ultimate paradox is the distinction of the divine essence and the divine energies. Both are uncreated, both are fully divine.... For the process theologians there is no essential problem about the transcendent God's activity in the world, for God is dually transcendent and there is distinction (but not division) between his primordial and his consequent natures ...as for the Eastern tradition, the point of ultimate incoherence is pushed back into the being of God himself.[24]

'Dually transcendent' may require a note: it refers to the contention, often stressed by Hartshorne, that God, according to this theory, surpasses all others on both his 'sides', both as infinite, independent, and eternal on the one and as finite, dependent, and temporal on the other. He is super-excellently all these things, but they are so distributed between the two 'sides' that, so it is claimed, there is no conflict, or, as Wiles puts it, no 'incoherence'. In my view, this contradicts man's awareness of God's *unity*. The Western tradition's difficulty, Wiles is saying, is that if God is pure act he can add nothing to himself. But doesn't the act of creating add something to him? I take him to be raising that question when he asks: 'How, then, is it that he creates?' For if it meant 'what would be the point of his creating?', the answer that he is super-generous would be too obvious. I have argued above, in agreement with Hartshorne, that it *would* add something to God, so contradicting his immutability (or perfection), if he created by an act of choice, but I have proposed instead that he is free in his creating in that absolute sense of freedom in which no

[24]*The Remaking of Christian Doctrine*, (S.C.M., 1974), pp. 108-110. Wiles refers here also to Karl Barth's paradoxical language about God as an instance of this procedure.

question of acting otherwise arises. It may now be clearer how important it is to show that Hartshorne's argument, directed against the doctrine of immutability, is valid if God's freedom in creating is interpreted in the usual way, but invalid on another, legitimate, interpretation.

Before we turn to the big question of the Eastern distinction between the divine essence and the divine energies, something should be said about Professor Wiles's own position. 'God', he writes, 'is not directly and irrefutably given', but to give up God 'would be to leave a whole area of human experience more opaque and inexplicable than it already is'. But he concludes: 'The infinite God is infinitely resistant to our systematizations'.[25] There are indeed limits to what we can say about God, and he is not 'irrefutably given' insofar as he can be avoided or merely 'suspected'. But unless we have *some* direct awareness of him, belief in him will not go beyond a more or less strong suspicion, so I would say. The process thinkers are in general agreement that God is to be discovered in all our thinking but only, it seems, in the form of a philosophical 'idea' found emerging from it or in that of a 'lure' towards moral values ('a power not ourselves, making for righteousness', in Matthew Arnold's words). The Christian spiritual tradition claims more than this: it holds, to repeat, that we can be aware of God as both our maker and our end, as both indescribably close to us and indescribably 'beyond' us. On the level of language there is plainly a paradox, but on the level of thought, of fundamental experience, there is a 'given'; nothing can contradict our own experience. What Wiles goes on to call 'the element of absurdity or incoherence' (which is hard to distinguish from a contradiction) appears only if this mysterious character of our experience is not recognized. My fear about Wiles's position, as here set out, is that what may seem no more than a suspicion of God, however strong, may seem also to lead into a real contradiction, in which case it would cease to be tenable. And if none of the attempts to

[25]P. 108.

speak coherently about 'relating God to the world' seems successful, it can hardly help much to say: 'Each has its points of strength and points of weakness. Each, if used critically, can rightly be used to illuminate differing aspects of our experience'.[26] Two black riddles cannot produce a white answer.

Talk about God's 'giving himself to us' must refer not to his bringing the world into existence (that would be 'emanationism') nor to the bare registration of a transcendent presence (which is what a purely 'natural' knowledge of God would seem to amount to) but to the forming of the personal relationship for which our own acceptance of it is required. This is the sphere of 'grace'. The theologians of the Eastern Orthodox Church say that Western talk about 'created grace' implies that it is not really *God* that we know, and it cannot be denied that Thomist writing has been for long hesitant and unsatisfactory about this. But they insist further that we must speak of 'divinization' and that God is knowable in one sense (the divine 'energies') but in another completely unknowable (the divine 'essence'). In the paragraph quoted from him originally, Wiles cites Vladimir Lossky's *The Vision of God* as follows: 'The divine nature must be called at the same time incommunicable and in a sense communicable; we attain participation in the nature of God, yet he remains totally inaccessible. We must preserve both things at once and must preserve the antinomy as the criterion of piety'. I have suggested[27] that there is no need to speak of an 'antinomy'. Again, it seems to me, we can consult our fundamental experience and find that we are aware of God himself (an awareness of what is not God *himself* can be only an awareness of something else) but that our awareness is a very limited one. An abstract idea of the Infinite may well seem incompatible with finite knowledge of it. But the knowledge of God which is available for us declares itself to be limited, and we must simply take it as such.

[26]P. 111.
[27]*The Absolute and the Atonement*, (Allen and Unwin, 1971), pp. 216-218.

It may be objected that 'knowledge' of God is not enough, for we 'participate' in his nature, and that is what is meant by 'divinization'. It has been often remarked that 'participation' is the most slippery word in the metaphysical vocabulary, and it should be sufficient to say that we cannot *share* anything with God in the sense of having anything strictly in *common* with him. 'Divinization', it is surely obvious, cannot be taken in the bald literal sense. Time after time one can find Christian writers using this language with enthusiasm and eventually remarking, as if by an afterthought, that of course it does not mean *identification* with God. It means assimilation to God, *union* with him, and I venture to say that it would be better always to use this word instead of continuing to scandalize metaphysicians (Protestant ones, in particular). Knowledge, which in this context is at the same time love, *is* union, for Western scholastic thinkers among others, although their doctrine of 'intentional union' is not put to full use in the present connection. When we become aware of anything around us, we are finding it present to our sense-organs: we are directly aware of our own bodies and so also of other bodies, as acting upon them, for the cause is present, in this way of thinking, *in* the effect. We are aware of nettles *in* the discomfort which they cause when we touch them, although we know them only as objects which do that sort of thing. Even in so trivial a matter as this, there is an awareness of the *other* as present to the mind; it is found as present to the body, but it is the mind that does the finding, making the object present to itself. This basic fact about our experience is pregnant with meaning. It is so far from true that a trivial incident can have no implications for our knowledge of God, that the union of the mind with the other which it exemplifies is a foreshadowing of our union with God. The human mind at all levels functions as it does because it is made for union with God. An awareness even of nettles makes some difference to the state of one's mind, but no difference to the nettles. This is a union without confusion. A union in this sense of human persons, a loving intimacy, makes a great difference to both of them, but there is no confusion of persons. The union of the human mind with God makes the greatest possible difference to the human mind, but God is still unchanged.

Wiles put the question whether God could give himself to his creation or 'is the "created grace" that he bestows something supernatural but less than himself?' It is the case that Western theology has discussed these matters in a way that suggests these questions. If 'grace' means 'God acting on us', then it is uncreated. If it refers to the effect of his action in us, then it is created. If it means the *union* between God and man, it makes no sense to say either that it is created or that it is uncreated. And it is absurd to suggest that there is some half-way house between God and man (Karl Rahner has spoken of a 'quasi-formal union'). Nor is 'grace' a third something in which they meet. The answer, I am suggesting, is that God does give himself, in the loving knowledge of him which he makes possible for us. The 'graced' man is still a limited creature, although what he knows is God himself. It is hardly surprising, in view of our littleness, that such a knowledge can begin in a very small way. Here we have to speak in figures, which for some may be meaningless. But it can hardly be without significance that they have been meaningful for so many down the ages.

In the last few paragraphs I have been stating my own opinions pretty freely because I have had difficulty in finding others in this area which seem intelligible, but I should be happy to receive correction. As I see it, the Christian tradition has always claimed that we can have a knowledge of God which is not just a matter of philosophical speculation but one of personal relationship. But in the West it has been for long closely associated with a philosophical system, Thomist Aristotelianism, which cannot consistently allow of such a thing. Now that Thomism is no longer the reigning philosophy, one may hope that traditional Christians will find better ways of expressing themselves on this vital matter. I shall return to the topic in the final chapter.

IV
Fellow-Travellers

The recently appointed F. D. Maurice Professor at
King's College (London), Keith Ward, begins his book
Rational Theology and the Creativity of God[1] by distinguishing
two main ways in which 'the traditional philosophical idea
of God' has been interpreted:

> In one tradition, which may be termed the tradition of 'in-
> clusive infinity', God has been understood as including all
> possible and actual things within himself. One might mention
> Plotinus, Ramanuja, Spinoza, Hegel, and Whitehead as belong-
> ing to this tradition. The whole universe is an expression, or
> emanation, of the unlimited reality of God, or the Absolute;
> he includes it within his being, though he is not limited by its
> finite forms.

It seems necessary to pause at this point to consider how
these statements are to be interpreted. The suggestion
might seem to be that God is considered, by all the thinkers
named above, to be himself in process of development.
Some writers in this tradition say that there is really
only the One Reality, of which finite things are the
'appearances'; that has been regarded by the Christian
tradition as confusedly identifying the finite with the infinite or as involving the conclusion that the finite is in fact
illusory. As I understand Whitehead, for him God includes
the finite in the sense that he has a finite 'side' himself to
which the world continually contributes, but the finite

[1]Published by Basil Blackwell, Oxford, 1982.

does not simply emanate from him. The passage quoted continues as follows:

> The other tradition may be called the tradition of 'exclusive infinity'; in being infinite, God excludes all finite things from himself. He is fully real in himself alone; no addition of finite realities to him can really be an addition, since he is already infinite; so the world is neither necessary to God, nor does it make any difference to his unlimited reality. The most influential exponent of this tradition is Aquinas, though Descartes, Leibnitz, and Kant, together with most Christian theologians, also belong to it.[2]

We have met this in principle already in connection with Hartshorne. God and creatures, I proposed, cannot be added together because they have nothing strictly in *common*. But now the question seems to have arisen: at the creation, when there was not only God but also the world, wasn't there an addition to reality? First, the question implies that there was a *time* before the creation; there has never been a *time*, I should reply, in which God can be said to have done anything, although the effects of his action are in time. This is incomprehensible in the precise sense that we cannot get our minds round it; but it is not meaningless, and there is no way of proving that this state of affairs is an impossibility. Second and perhaps even more important, when we say that something is a reality, that it is really there, we are asserting our knowledge of it, affirming it, claiming a relationship between ourselves and it. It does not follow that there is any relationship between the things that we affirm and one another. To affirm God and to affirm some part of his world is not to say that the one can be added to the other. And to say that God 'is fully real in himself alone', in an account of Christian theism, must not be taken to mean that there is something *un*real about his creatures.

Ward, as we should now expect, goes on at once to speak of 'a crucial difficulty which arises when the relation of

[2]P. 2.

God, the necessary, perfect and immutable being, to a universe of contingent, and even free, beings is considered ...the truly contingent cannot arise from the wholly necessary; and if creation, divine or human, is free and contingent, then creation is incompatible with necessity.... On this rock both traditional interpretations of theism founder'.[3] I have agreed that, if God's creating is thought to be free in the sense that it might not have occurred, then the argument holds, but not if it is taken to be an act of self-determining generosity. (It must be repeated here that the world is contingent upon God in the sense of being wholly dependent on him, and that the moral freedom of his creatures does not affect his immutability.) Clearly Ward regards his contention about God's creating as fundamental for his position as a whole, and this further justifies the importance which I have attached to dealing with it.[4] His conclusion follows immediately: what is required, he tells us, is 'not a rejection of the traditional idea of God, but a revision of it, utilizing an idea of infinity which may be called that of "dynamic infinity", a move which requires the admission of potency and temporality in God, but which can be reconciled with a properly interpreted doctrine of eternity and necessity'.

The main purpose of the book is a general defence of the view, set out on the first page, that 'the existence of God is the foundation of all being and value', and that 'belief in God is the highest expression of human rationality, and the guardian of our commitment to the ultimate value of human life and endeavour'. Here I must say at once that there is much in this defence which seems to me of great

[3]Pp. 2-3.

[4]Ward returns to the topic on several occasions; for instance he writes on p. 73: 'The old dilemma—either God's acts are necessary and therefore not free (could not be otherwise), or they are free and therefore arbitrary (nothing determines what they shall be)—has been sufficient to impale the vast majority of Christian philosophers down the ages'. For a different view compare, for instance, Père Louis Bouyer, *Cosmos*, (1982), p. 306: The freedom of God's love for us is 'only the other side of the deepest necessity of his nature'.

value.[5] Ward writes of the 'assumption or pre-orientation of the mind to assume that reality is rational' and argues that it 'can only be adequately substantiated if there exists one self-explanatory being which explains all others', going on to say: 'The traditional cosmological proofs of God can be interpreted as explorations of the idea of the intelligibility of the world'.[6] But he has to admit that there is no coercive proof of a self-explanatory being: it is always possible for someone to say that he sees no need for any such explanation. It is this state of affairs, among other things, that suggests to me that the quest for intelligibility would not get going at all unless there were already a 'suspicion' of an ultimate principle which is in fact present to the mind but not yet recognized as having anything to do with religion. It is the growth of this suspicion rather than rational considerations that leads to conviction in that case. It is the 'concept' of God, not the 'awareness' of him, that is Ward's concern in this book.

Some of his attacks on Thomism are, in my opinion, justified. But there is a good deal to be said about others, partly because they provide opportunities for clarifying a point of view which is fundamentally traditional but not uncritical. First I have to say that Ward is not always a safe guide to St Thomas's thinking. For instance, he writes: 'Aquinas follows the Aristotelian tradition of distinguishing the infinite sharply from the finite. . . . Thereby arises the doctrine of Divine Simplicity, and with it the total separation of God from the world. "Nothing can come into contact with God or partially intermingle with him in any way" (*Summa Theologiae*, qu. 3, art. 8)'.[7] The article referred

[5]To take a single example, the passage on belief in God as the guardian of morality (pp. 175-185) is perhaps the most effective discussion of the topic in print.

[6]P. 5.

[7]P. 71. Ward writes that it is possible, in his view, 'to admit a form of personal relationship in prayer which is impossible with the immutable, impassable [*sic*] God of Thomism', p. 87. Can he really believe that Thomists do not hold with such a relationship? I should agree that there are inconsistencies in Thomism and (which is far from being the same

to is headed 'whether God enters into composition with others', and the sense of 'composition' is seen in the reply that he cannot be either the formal or the material principle of what is not himself. The words quoted by Ward are themselves a quotation (from pseudo-Denis) and, literally translated, would read: 'There is no touching of him, that is, of God, nor any uniting such as to produce a mingling of parts'. Again, we read: 'The Thomist assertion that "the only genus to which God could belong would be the genus of existent" (qu. 3, art. 5) is incoherent. The class of "the existent" covers all actual things, not just God. Further, if one tries to speak of the purely, unrestrictedly existent, one ends with the absurdity that there exists something which has no other property than existing, that is, nothing'.[8] The passage quoted comes from a well-known discussion in which St Thomas concludes that God 'is not contained in any genus'. (Ward is aware of this—he mentions it on another page.) It is better translated: 'If God were in any genus, one would have to say that the genus would be [that of] being'—which is then shown to be incoherent. To speak of the 'unrestrictedly existent' is to speak of the infinite, which for Ward can be only potential, not actual.

We come to the heart of the difficulty with Ward's concept of God when, after remarking that 'God could not possess the necessary properties he does, unless he also possessed various contingent properties', he makes the following comment:

> Aquinas dimly saw this point when he insisted that God, though by his arguments he should have been the simple abstract form of Being, was in fact the most ceaselessly active

thing) in St Thomas. In an article in *Theological Studies*, March 1982, 'Does Process Theology Rest on a Mistake?' David B. Burrell speaks of 'Hartshorne's caricature of classical theism' (p. 409); the reply by Philip E. Devenish in the same place the following September seems to me ineffective. See also Burrell's *Aquinas, God and Action*, Routledge and Kegan Paul, 1979.

[8] P. 64.

of all beings. But it is precisely that notion of activity that Thomism cannot in the end allow for. The idea of perfection which is used is that of something static, which cannot change on pain of becoming something worse. So the Thomist God must be immutable and supremely active at the same time, a feat beyond even the capacity of omnipotence.[9]

How can Ward account for the delighted acceptance of this alleged real contradiction by so many intelligent thinkers and so many famous mystics? Just as freedom and necessity are formally contradictories on the human level but can be *thought* as convergent at infinity, so too with rest and activity. There is no real contradiciton between them in God, for in him what is thinkable as positive is present and what is thinkable only as deficiency is absent. Thus what is positive about rest, for us, is fulfilment, satisfaction, but it is not accompanied in God, as it is for us, by inactivity. On the contrary, he is infinitely active. Such talk can only point to an apprehension of God which is the well-spring of religion. For rationalists who deal only in abstract ideas and sense-data this must be meaningless.

This is the place for noting that, according to Ward, 'there is no total sum of eternal ideas, but a constantly changing stock of imaginatively created ideas, limited only by God's character as wise, good and loving.... If one is clear that possibles only exist insofar as they are conceived by the Divine mind, then it causes no difficulty that God should come to conceive new things—as long as he can change'.[10] He must go on changing indefinitely for Ward, it seems, on pain of death. I have argued for the rejection of possible worlds. If this is God's one world, then he has a plan for it (which includes our moral freedom and is to that extent at risk) which he will constantly further. Ward continues: 'The Creator will not only be ignorant of what will be actual in the future, that he does not decree; he will not know everything that is possible. Nevertheless, this is by no means a defect in God; for if anything becomes

[9]P. 160.
[10]P. 154.

possible, he makes it so, and this "limitation" alone makes free creativity in God possible. To say that something is positively possible is to say that it is conceived by God, so he knows everything positively possible'. This notion of God's first making something possible by conceiving it and then creating it seems to me another case of an unacceptable anthropomorphism. We cannot talk of *how* God creates. Creation is 'out of nothing'. We can only register the fact: 'God spoke and it was made'. The chief importance of the passage lies rather in showing how much store Ward sets on 'free creativity' as a sort of spontaneous growth. I can understand that a secular humanist might consider this 'free creativity' an ultimate value, an ideal, for himself and his fellows, but it seems strange for a theist to insist upon it as a characteristic of the divine life.

It may be becoming clearer that the process theology view of God as everlasting in the sense of timeful, leads to conclusions which are hard to envisage. Ward accepts that, according to his view, 'there are times at which God exists'. He goes on: 'This in turn entails that God does not create those times; he cannot logically create a condition of his own existing. Time becomes a property of God. . . . One has the image of temporality as a sort of abstract universal, independent of God and limiting his unrestricted being. . . . Such universals are necessarily parts of the being of God, not at all independent of him'.[11] I hope that the reader will think that this speaks for (or rather against) itself. On the next page Ward faces the difficulty that 'we must think of the Divine time as running in parallel with human time' yet 'it seems that one cannot say that God is simultaneous with all events in the universe at a given time, since there is no absolute time'. So Ward proposes that 'God must exist in a number of different time-sequences, not relatable to each other by relations of absolute simultaneity. . . he may be said to be present at every created time, though not confined to it'. This might lead one to conclude that God must be simply *beyond* time. But Ward concludes: 'God

[11]P. 163.

is temporal, in that he does some things before he does others, and, in changing, he projects his being along one continuous, temporal path. But there may be many such paths...God must be conceived as moving along all such paths...'.[12] Surely there *must* be innumerable such paths. But we cannot be expected to take seriously such excursions into science fiction.

Ward does not seem to grasp the importance of negative language as a 'pointer' to the divine life. He remarks that 'one cannot be satisfied with wholly negative statements, for that would leave God as a mere nothing'.[13] This suggests that he does not realize what people are doing when they use this language: they are claiming an awareness of God which is non-conceptual (although it gives rise to concepts which 'point' to it). This is the point of talk about 'beyondness', for instance. Ward quotes Erigena's statement that 'super-essential' refers to what is 'more than essence' and comments: 'That "more than" adds an important element to sheer negation; it says that it is not inappropriate to call God wise even though he is more than we can conceive by the word "wise".'[14] But at this point, when he seemed to be moving in the right direction, he drops the topic with the remark that 'it is hardly an acceptable escape from the incoherence of a wholly ineffable being to add to it the incoherence of a being of whom all attributes can be affirmed at once, and aver that the truth lies in the paradox formed by the combination of two incoherences'.

It is significant that his approximation to a notion of the Trinity, mentioned in connection with 'the Plotinian Triad of the One, the Intellect, and the World-Shaper' is a 'more purely internalized triad within the Divine Being, of the self-existent, the exemplary Ideal, and the appreciative awareness of it'.[15] I call this an 'approximation' to a notion

[12] P. 166.
[13] P. 61.
[14] P. 62.
[15] P. 233.

of the Trinity, because he says that it 'is, perhaps, more like some accounts of the Christian doctrine of a Divine Trinity' [than the Plotinian Triad]. In the only other place where he touches on the Trinity, he rejects the idea of 'a sort of committee of gods, loving each other', on the ground that, if there can be 'only one self-determining being, the hypothesis is ruled out as incoherent, anyway'. He dismisses the suggestion that the Trinity is a sort of social reality, that there are three persons (centres of awareness) in one substance, for 'in addition to the fact that this conflicts with all traditional views of the Trinity, it is clear that a person is a substance, and that it is one being who is omnipotent, not a society of persons'.[16] He is surprisingly ignorant of what has gone on and is going on among traditional theologians. It was the regular traditional, patristic, doctrine that the persons possessed those characteristics of human personality which do not of themselves imply limitation (a notion which I have discussed earlier in this book). It was the influence of Augustine which led to an account which suggests something more like the psychological unfolding of a single person. St Thomas, although at first keeping to the tradition, allowed himself to be influenced by the popular Augustinianism in this matter, and the notion of the Trinity as three 'modes' of God is still widely current. It is, however, not only perfectly orthodox but becoming increasingly common for theologians to say that God *is* three persons in the sense that Father, Son, and Holy Spirit are *interdependent* (the Father could not be the Father without the Son and the Holy Spirit; likewise the Son and the Holy Spirit could not be *who* they are without the other two persons). There is no logical difficulty about the claim that three persons interdependent in this sense are *absolutely* united. This is the traditional *perichoresis*, 'circumincession', an eternal movement of love, which is also compatible with the traditional doctrine of the Son's 'proceeding' from the Father and the

[16]P. 86.

Holy Spirit's 'proceeding' from the Father through the Son.[17]

Like many other writers who are influenced to a greater or lesser extent by process theology, Ward sees that Whitehead's God is not really a creator at all, and it is therefore Hartshorne's dipolar God who is offered to us at the end of the book as the alternative to the absurdities which we have been asked to observe in the Thomist (not to be identified with the traditional) theology. But Ward is not to be described as a process theologian without qualification. Indeed I think that he ought not to be described as a process theologian at all but as a fellow-traveller with process theologians. For he maintains the doctrine of personal immortality, and in his account, although I have had to disagree with it on many occasions, God is, at least on one 'side' of him, what I would venture to call the God of religion (which I could not say about Hartshorne's God without serious danger of misleading). Ward's introduction into God of change, time, development and so forth is, I believe, a most serious mistake, but it is not incompatible with personal belief in the Father of Jesus Christ.

It remains to substantiate some of these remarks by a few references to the book's last chapter. 'God', we read, 'is thus the absolutely originative creator, not the passive container of process philosophy; but the one who is uniquely and immutably self-existent, and is ontologically prior to all beings other than himself'.[18] We are told that 'one may see God as necessary in his eternal nature, and also as contingent in the everlastingly temporal acts by which he expresses that nature' and that if one rejects Whitehead's view that the ultimate metaphysical truth is atomism... and if one is not convinced that substances can be reduced to processes, there is nothing against one's

[17]This is discussed by Louis Bouyer, *Le Consolateur*, (Les Editions du Cerf, Paris, 1980), esp. p. 268. (English ed. to be published by St. Bede's Publ.) Cf. *A Dictionary of Christian Theology*, (ed. Richardson), p. 350.

[18]P. 322. 'Passive container', however, would not be accepted as a proper description of Whitehead's God by his adherents.

accepting that there is a God 'who freely decides to create beings other than himself'.[19] What remains unacceptable for a traditional Christian in Ward's theology is conveniently summed up in the following passage: 'The unsatisfactoriness of dualistic views of the relation between God and the world may be overcome by stressing the decisive change in the being of God which finite creation occasions, and the ideal consummation of unity-in-diversity towards which creation moves.... He is involved in the history of finite creation, as it is indeed a phase in his own development and the determination of his own being as self-giving love'.[20] Here the theory of a changing 'side' in God may seem to be leading to an ultimate *merging* of the Creator with his creatures. The contrast between 'inclusive infinity' and 'exclusive infinity' with which the book began took no account of a relationship between God and man, that of *union*, in which there is all that man can desire while there is no confusion between finite and infinite. For Ward's views on life after earthly death and on the suffering of God (both touched on cursorily in this book) we may turn to another published a few months later.

In his *Holding Fast to God*[21] Ward has replied with great effectiveness to Don Cupitt's *Taking Leave of God*, but he has also gone over in a less technical way a good deal of the ground covered in the previous book. There is a whole chapter on immortality. 'A Christian', he points out, 'is committed to belief in immortality, for two main reasons: the existence of a God of love and the resurrection of Jesus. The whole life of faith is one of trusting that the love which we fitfully apprehend in this life will be clearly seen hereafter'.[22] A good deal of the chapter is devoted to arguing that 'we could continue to exist as the same people, even in a different space-time from this one, and in a body

---

[19]P. 230.

[20]P. 233. It must be added that Ward goes on at once to stress 'the autonomy and reality of finite agents' as against 'monist' views.

[21]S.P.C.K., 1982.

[22]P. 120.

which was different in significant ways from these physical bodies'.[23] But eventually we are told that 'Christians speak of heaven as being in love with God.... We may suppose that, if we are truly and fully in love with him (because he fills us with his love, and we gladly allow him to do so), we will not notice the passing of time...'.[24] But such love presupposes vision, and the traditional account of heaven as the adoration of God, the entering into the riches of his beauty, is still, I think, a valid 'pointer'. An extended quotation from the third chapter is necessary to show Ward's view of suffering in God:

> God suffers with and for his creatures, so that he might make them one with him. But how can God be blissful and suffer at the same time? Much traditional theology has been unable to face this question, and has denied that God really suffers— but then, the doctrine of the cross becomes very hard to understand. What we have to say is that God is supremely happy in the contemplation of those values which he possesses in his own being. He is happy in those values which are being realized in the world. These sorts of happiness are overwhelmingly greater than even the whole sum of the sorrows of the world. Nevertheless, God does share in the sufferings of creatures; and he transmutes these sufferings into forms of happiness which are shaped by them. The sufferings are not just forgotten or swamped by joy; they are used creatively to produce particular forms of experience, which do not just express a self-satisfied pleasure, but rather a complex of feelings which include sorrow, but express overall a deep satisfaction, in seeing that sorrow used, negated and overcome. The happiness of God, we might say, is not the innocent pleasure of a child; it is the deep and unshakable joy of the Christ, who has been crucified but is now glorified and who has transfigured sorrow into a richer apprehension of final well-being.[25]

---

[23]P. 124.

[24]P. 128. The last part of the chapter is concerned with showing that 'non-bodily existence is conceivable', but Ward adds: 'An after-world more commensurate with our more mundane and undeveloped spirits would be the resurrection-world postulated by Christian faith' (p. 133).

[25]P. 37.

The last suggestion seems to be that there are some deep joys which are impossible without previous sorrows overcome, and this is said to be true not only of ourselves but also of God. Here it is necessary to distinguish the human consciousness of Jesus from the divine consciousness of the Word, the Second Person of the Trinity. It is no part of the traditional doctrine of the cross that the divine Word was crucified and died in his divine 'nature' (the Council of Chalcedon explicitly rejected that). According to the regular formula, the Son of God died 'in his human nature', and this means, so we are told by leading Catholic theologians, that the man Jesus was united with the divine Son in a unique way called a 'personal' one: he is the perfect human expression of the divine Son, in that sense his perfect 'instrument', as St Thomas puts it, the head of the race, the Lord of the world. Failure to appreciate this fundamental distinction is very common and far from unknown even among academic theologians. The passage quoted is not by a long way the only one in this book in which Ward appeals to the doctrine of the cross as justifying an insistence that God suffers. The picture of the world's sorrows shared by God but overwhelmed by his happiness is an anthropomorphism which I find quite implausible. We cannot properly surmise what it can be like to have God's consciousness. But we can say that suffering is a limitation and can therefore have no place in God. The description of a 'complex of feelings' is a transference of a human psychological state to the realm of the divine in a way for which I can see no justification. Process theologians commonly follow Hartshorne in requiring a 'strict analogy' between God and man with results that many Christian believers must find horrifying.

This is the point at which to say something about the statement frequently made by process theologians that the traditional view of 'analogy' has 'broken down'. The fact of the matter is that a doctrine of analogy is to be found in obsolescent Thomist textbooks which purported to function as a sort of bridge between finite and infinite: I am not the only traditional theologian to hold that analogical language, properly understood, is the language which we find ourselves using when we say, in the light of our faith, that, for example, God knows and loves us.[26] The non-conceptual awareness of God which is at the heart of faith reveals him to us as the utterly transcendent but at the same time as knowing and loving us in a way of which our way of knowing and loving is seen to be but a feeble derivative. It is the same to say that to talk of God's knowing and loving us is to use 'pointing' language. Analogical language is a consequence of faith, not a device proving something to unbelievers.

To return to the passage under discussion, the latter part of it is a description of what human beings can make of their sufferings in certain circumstances. It presupposes that they can be used for good. Are we to think that God's sufferings do *him* good? If they are caused by human sin, there is no guarantee, in this account, that they must prove to benefit anyone. I have argued earlier that the denial of suffering in God does not mean that he has no concern for his creatures; he has an infinite, unchangeable, concern for them. Ward also tells us, in reference to God, that 'once such a being had created a world with suffering in it, it is surely more perfect to sympathize with and share in that suffering than to remain indifferent to it' and that 'he freely chooses to share in our suffering, precisely so that he can help us, not by force, but by sympathy and the persuasion of love'.[27] But God is not 'indifferent': he is always offering what is best for us. This picture of God's turning on his own suffering seems to me to make this thesis even harder to accept. And it is not as though we could be aware of his sufferings in sympathy for us. What we can be aware of, I would say, is simply his love. Perhaps the passage refers once more just to 'the doctrine of the cross'. Certainly the cross *manifests* God's love for us in the

[26]For instance, J. D. Robert, O.P. in *Nouvelle Revue Théologique*, May-July 1983, *'Dieu sans l'être'*, p. 409 and E. L. Mascall, *The Openness of Being*, (Darton Longman and Todd), pp. 33-34.

[27]P. 118.

sufferings of Jesus, the perfect human expression of the divine Son. But that is another matter.

At the end of the Introduction to this book, Professor Ward candidly remarks: 'My attack upon Cupitt is also an attack upon a clearer and more uncompromising version of my former self', and this gives a peculiar force to many passages which I should have liked to quote. He also refers to a book of his, *The Concept of God*, written in 1974, which, he says, was 'very much influenced by the sorts of views Cupitt holds', and he tells us that he has 'come to believe in the necessity for a much more positive account of the nature of God which will be true to a mature Christian faith'. I hope that it will not be thought offensive for me to say what is in my mind, that I look forward to his working process theology out of his system[28] and giving us another book which could be one of quite extraordinary usefulness.

In this chapter I am concerned with those who combine the profession of Christianity with the adoption of the process theology doctrine of a changing and suffering God. They would claim, of course, that Christianity, properly understood, supports this doctrine. It seems to me that the history of Christianity and the history of religion in general are against them; that is an appeal to religious experience, which will not be accepted unless the experience in question is shared. Here I can only urge that it can be shared. For Roman Catholics in America, the most influential of the fellow-travellers, I gather, is Fr David Tracy. In his well-known book *Blessed Rage for Order* he writes as follows of Professor Hartshorne: 'To my knowledge, no other single writer in modernity has proposed as

---

[28]Traditional Christians reading Ward's book may not always realize that process theology lies behind certain passages. For instance, Ward rightly points out the danger that 'we may come to think of God as adjectival to the world, as just one aspect or part of a wider reality, which could not exist without the world' (p. 105), but goes on to say: 'God is the whole; he is the infinite, outside whom there is nothing. He does include the world in his being, though he need not have done so'. To use the language of 'inclusion' here, as Hartshorne does, could suggest the *disappearance* of finite beings into God.

carefully formulated and evidential a series of alternatives to the classical dilemmas of theists and non-theists alike'.[29] That implies, I take it, that he is thought to have disposed of non-theists' objections to theism. At this stage it is not necessary for me to rehearse my objections to Hartshorne's special positions. 'Process thought', Tracy also writes, 'is a consistent and systematic theological option which has developed almost exclusively in our own highly empirical Anglo-American culture. Here is a position which gives no mere lip service to modernity's demand for radical critique, fundamental change, and personal responsibility'. I wonder whether 'highly empirical' should read 'anti-metaphysical'; and if 'modernity' demands changing everything for the sake of changing it, then it shows a sad misunderstanding of personal responsibility, which the Christian tradition has always insisted upon, even though many Christians (it should not need saying) have often been so slack about it.

'My own suspicion', Tracy says later on, 'is that all authentic Christians live and pray as if God were really affected by their action. They live as if, to use the expression of one process theologian, God really were Pure Unbounded Love struggling, suffering, achieving with humanity'. Why should it not be possible that it is part of God's providence for us to be able, for instance, to help others by our prayers without his being made to change his mind or involve himself in a time-series in order to answer them? No doubt there are plenty of 'authentic Christians' who have a picture in their minds of a vaguely anthropomorphic figure who intervenes from time to time in the world's affairs. But I very much doubt whether many of them would say that they picture God as 'struggling'. I doubt too whether many of them would be happy with Tracy's statement about God (even if expressed in simpler language) that 'the dipolar God as eminently temporal may be understood to be in a continued process of self-creation,

---

[29]P. 174. The quotations which follow will be found in the course of the same eighth chapter.

again analogous to the self's own temporal creation'. In our time it is becoming rapidly less and less possible to take God for granted, and my conviction is that anthropomorphic language of this kind is going to be more and more off-putting. If there really is a Creator, people will say, he must be unimaginably different from us and the beauties and horrors of our world.

I must confine myself now to fellow-travellers who publish in my own part of the world, omitting all reference to followers of Karl Barth, for whom the suffering of God is vouched for by the Bible, although it seems to me very desirable that they should face up to the enormous difficulties which this view involves. *Trinity and Temporality* by Fr John J. O'Donnell, S.J. has appeared from the Oxford University Press with the subtitle 'The Christian Doctrine of God in the Light of Process Theology and the Theology of Hope'. This is a clearly written and usefully informative work, concentrating on Schubert Ogden and Jürgen Moltmann, which argues in its first chapter that modern atheism has as its basis the suffering of the world: we are told that 'Christian theology must be able to formulate its doctrine of God in such a way that it takes account of the sufferings of the world. . . . Classical philosophical theism's apathetic God could only intensify the question. A revolution in the concept of God will surely point in the direction of a God who participates in the suffering of his creation'.[30] I can only say that I know a good many unbelievers (probably not really atheists) who would find such a revolution an additional obstacle to their believing in God and that it is not made clear to me why a suffering God should be considered advantageous for anyone. At the end of the book we read: 'The Christian does not have a

---

[30]*Op. cit.*, p. 23. Stangely the book repeats many of the process writers' misconceptions of traditional theology, but the author is anxious to be fair. It is pointed out, for instance (p. 18), that Walter Stokes ('Is God Really Related to the World?' in *Proceedings of the American Catholic Philosophical Association*, p. 39) proposed that God's act of creating is both free as self-determination and identical with his 'essence'.

speculative solution to the problem of suffering. What he does have is a story to relate, a gospel about how God came to us in our suffering...the history of the suffering of the world goes on and refutes all our systems. Beyond all our reasons, however, lies another argument, that of our discipleship itself...such praxis will be in the final analysis the most convincing argument, for this age or any other, of the truth of the Christian experience of God'.[31] Yes, but we all knew that anyway. And the 'freewill defence' does cope in principle with the problem of evil.

Two articles which have appeared recently, one in *The Irish Theological Quarterly*,[32] the other in *The Clergy Review*[33] (British), I must suppose to be written by fellow-travellers. In the former, the writer, Mary T. Rattigan, announces in the introductory paragraph: 'The notion of a suffering God...is a central insight associated with this theological perspective'. After a remarkably readable and reliable account of process thought, that of Hartshorne in particular, the author concludes with a section headed 'Divine Suffering', I quote from the opening paragraph:

> The process understanding is that God suffers the consequence of being a participant in the history of the world. Everything that happens enters the divine life as a felt experience of goodness or loss.... To support the judgment that God truly suffers, process theologians have turned their attention to the biblical narratives. Daniel Day Williams represents one such effort to elucidate the claim that God suffers on the basis of biblical testimony.... The history of Israel suggests that God was affected by both the acceptance and the rejection of his people.

It seems strange to me that process thinkers, even when they are Christians, should accept quite literally what we read about God's feelings in the Old Testament. If the Old Testament is to be taken as an authority for God's

[31]Pp. 202-203.
[32]1982, no. 3, 'The Concept of God in Process Thought'.
[33]Oct. 1978, 'God, Time and Change'. I replied in detail to this article in the same place the following January.

sufferings, it is presumably to be taken as an authority for his flying into tempers, ordering massacres and indulging in undignified conversations with various Old Testament characters. And since, on the process account of things, God's consciousness is in everlasting time, we have again the intolerable picture of his joys and sorrows piling up for ever. The paragraph continues later, summarizing Williams's views:[34]

> As Jesus suffered in his love with and for sinners he revealed the suffering love of God, namely, how God enters into and takes into himself the situation created by the sins of human beings. By saying that God suffers in the sufferings of Jesus [he] does not mean, however, that God experiences the physical pain or mental anguish of Jesus' death. Rather it means that God feels the experience of that suffering which could only belong to Jesus himself. . . . God not only suffers with us but *for* us. The main concern here is to focus on the redemptive aspect of suffering, the ability of suffering love to effect reconciliation, to bring about the transformation Christians call 'the new creation'.

In other words, presumably, God empathizes with this suffering of Jesus. The suffering of Jesus, I would say, profits us because in his leading a sinless life in the world he found himself faced with a cruel death as the way to his Father and to the power to unite us with him which he has in his risen life. Suffering was a necessary means to this end. But how, I was asking just now, would divine suffering help us? Here we have an answer offered:

> He [Williams] developed an explanation of how a personal awareness that God endures our suffering can be redemptive by using a model supplied by psychotherapy. The transformation which takes place in the therapeutic situation is proposed as an analogue for comprehending how God's suffering love can act as a transforming power in the world. . . . The consciousness that God suffers with us in our failures and losses can bring about personal healing and re-creation. . .our personal faith experiences, especially those of prayer and wor-

[34]We are referred to his book, *The Spirit and Forms of Love*, p. 166.

ship, often resonate with a process God who is truly moved by our joys and our sufferings.

Before commenting on this, I should like to refer to the other article mentioned above. In this, Santiago Sia, after giving another very useful account of Hartshorne's position, warned that we must 'analyze the very meaning of perfection' before applying it to God. It seems to me that here and in the passage about Williams just quoted the same mistake is made, that we find God in ourselves in the sense that any human experience which we find valuable is to be attributed as it stands to him. Traditional thought makes a distinction between those experiences which have negative characteristics associated with them and those which are purely positive. Only the latter can be attributed to God and only in that analogical way to which I have already referred. We find God in ourselves not just in certain of our own experiences (we are not aware of him as *sharing* them) but as the super-person *whom* we experience as knowing and loving us in his own transcendent way. Again I would suggest that what we can be aware of is simply God's love and that it is a mistake, a very natural one, to associate with that love the limitations which attach to interhuman relationships. Hartshorne would say that it is the 'very meaning' of perfection that one should go on getting better and better (therefore God must always be 'surpassing himself') and that one should be distressed when those whom we love are distressed (and therefore God must be). The awareness of God, I should reply, gives us an extended meaning of 'love', an inkling of the divine love or 'perfection' which is wholly *for us* but undergoes no change in consequence, no diminution of its absolute joy. No one denies that this is in the highest degree mysterious for us. But for God to be incapable of suffering, or rather for suffering to be unable to touch him, is not a contradiction, and the claim that only a suffering God is 'religiously adequate' is rejected by the tradition as just the reverse of the truth. Traditional theologians today show a notable unanimity in seeing the redemption to lie in unity with Christ, in the fruits of the resurrection. According to one of the Collects, in every Mass 'the work of the redemption comes into effect'. So here we have a head-on collision between process thinkers' claims about our experience of God and traditional ones.

It is now becoming usual once more to say that Christian doctrine is 'the crystallization of Christian experience'. *Lex orandi, lex credendi* may be understood in that sense. So the teaching of the classical Christian mystics is of great importance, in particular on the question whether sorrow can enter the divine consciousness. We may call on von Hügel as a witness to their answer. In his address, 'Suffering and God', after speaking of God as 'perfect love' and 'unmixed joy', he goes on: 'I believe this to be a true account of the fundamental religious experience and apprehension. But if so, we will not admit the presence of any Evil, be it Sin or even only Sorrow, be they actual or only potential, in him who dwarfs for us all our little human goodness and earthly joy by his utter Sanctity and sheer Beatitude'.[35] And I must make my own, even at the risk of causing offence, the words of Père Paul Galtier: 'To make out that fear, disgust and sadness overflowed from Christ's human nature into his divine nature has always seemed an impiety; for anyone in our time to want this spectacle to unfold in the divine consciousness itself, so as to seem moving to us, indicates moreover a profound ignorance of what the Christian life has always been'.[36] In the same place Galtier wrote: 'People imagine a Christ who is accessible even in his divine being to what makes men weak and wretched. That is to return to certain morbid dreams of other days.... Men love to recognize themselves in their

---

[35] *Essays and Addresses*, p. 209. On p. 188 he remarks that only such a view 'could defend and transmit the very deepest note of the religious consciousness'. Eastern Orthodox theologians sometimes speak of suffering in God, but they can hardly claim as traditional a vew that receives no countenance from the Cappadocian Fathers on whom they usually and rightly rely.

[36] *L'Unité du Christ*, 1939, p. 327. This must not be taken to mean that I should endorse Galtier's Christology on all points.

Saviour, but a God so degraded could not move them'. Galtier, of course, could use the prescribed formula 'the Son of God suffered' because the divine Word 'appropriated to himself' the sufferings of his flesh and of his soul, his 'instruments'.

Finally, I must return to Fr W. Norris Clarke's important essay 'Christian Theism and Whiteheadian Process Philosophy: Are They Compatible?' in his book *The Philosophical Approach to God* of which I have already made much use. Earlier work of his had made it clear to many that traditional theology in general, and that of St Thomas in particular, cannot be rightly charged with presenting to us a God who is indifferent to what goes on in his world. Here he exploits the advantage gained to show that Whiteheadians and traditional theologians have more in common than is generally realized, and he urges them with great courtesy, tact and skill to reconsider some of their positions, allowing that traditional theologians need to reconsider some of their own. He himself offers Whiteheadians certain modifications of statements currently found in what can be called 'official Thomism'. To express the truth that God's knowledge and love of his world do not change him, it has been customary to say, as we have seen, that God has 'no real relation to the world'. Clarke therefore makes the sensible suggestion that this language should be 'quietly dropped' and that we should without hesitation say that 'God is really and truly related to the world in the order of his personal consciousness'.[37] He now faces the question whether 'the personal relation of love between God and men can properly be called a mutual relation' and replies that God 'receives love from us and experiences joy *precisely because* of our response: in a word, that his consciousness is contingently and qualitatively *different* because of what we do'. This, however, he goes on, remains 'on the level of God's relational consciousness and therefore does not involve increase or decrease in the infinite Plenitude of God's *intrinsic inner being* and perfection.... God does not

[37]*Op. cit.,* p. 91.

become a more or less perfect being because of the love we return to him or the joy he experiences thereat (or its absence)'.[38] I should like to add to this the consideration that what we speak of, correctly, as 'our' responses are nevertheless simply God's gifts to us which we could have refused; we have no initiative, in regard to God, in accepting from him, but only (negatively) in refusing his gifts, as I have earlier suggested. God sees and loves us as the recipients of his gifts. He is the sole source of all that is good.

If I understand Clarke's doctrine of secondary causality, what I am saying here does not fit in with it. I cannot speak, as he proceeds to do, of a 'mutual giving and receiving' that is part of 'God's relational consciousness'. If what the Whiteheadians want is that we should be able to produce something for God's benefit from resources not actuated by him, even if they were to grant that these resources were created by him, then, it seems to me, we should have to reply that this was just not on. The voice of tradition, as I hear it, tells me that we are *always* at the receiving end in our relations with God. I have no right to demand that others should hear it that way, but I should be ready to go on talking about it to them for as long as they were ready to listen. Clarke adds: 'To receive love as a person, as we better understand the unique logic of interpersonal relations today, is not at all an imperfection, but precisely a dimension of the *perfection of personal being* as lovingly responsive.... Our concept of God is bound to be open to partial evolution as our own understanding evolves as to what it means to be a person...'. I doubt whether we have an understanding of what it means to be a person which is superior to that of the great contemplatives of the past. And the whole enterprise of discovering, without reference to God, what 'perfection' means and then applying the result to him seems to me a mistake. Clarke has said such excellent things about God's *Infinite Perfection* (his italics) that I am puzzled by what he writes here. So I cannot go along with his 'further concession' to the White-

[38]P. 92.

headians that God may be called 'not just the Supreme
Cause of the world, but equally if not more so the Supreme
Effect, in the sense of being the Supreme *Receiver* from all
things that exist . . .'.[39] When Clarke turns to the charge
that his concessions imply that there are in God the tem-
porally successive states on which process thinkers insist, I
find myself in my usual admiring agreement with what he
says. But he is not content to show that 'a non-temporal
view of the divine relational consciousness is *one* viable
metaphysical option'. He suggests that 'if change is restricted to the relational dimension of God's consciousness, we can rethink the concept of change so that it is seen
to involve no imperfection at all'.[40] For it would leave God's
'inner plenitude' untouched. But he accepts that this would
require for God 'His own unique mode of time-succession
correlated with ours'.[41] Here he adds that 'God knows
what we are doing by how he allows his power, in itself
indeterminate, to flow through us; by how we determi-
nately channel this flow of power, according to our own
free initiatives. Thus he knows not by being acted on, but
through his own action in us'. This I can accept insofar as,
in creating us free beings, God, as it were, commits himself
to empowering the physical actions which we perform,
even when they result from a refusal of the good alternative which he offers us. But that does not square with a
'mutual giving and receiving'. By the admission that there
may be 'time' (in some sense) in God, Clarke finds himself
faced by the question whether God in his 'relational consciousness' is 'truly *growing* . . . thus in some significant way
finite'. That I cannot accept. It suggests that the 'relational
consciousness' is somehow separate from the 'rest' of the
divine consciousness. God's timeless knowledge of the
finite, I would say, does not make him in any way finite. I
cannot accept Clarke's concession to the Whiteheadians
that 'the infinite, remaining infinite, can still be "enriched"

[39]P. 93.
[40]P. 95.
[41]P. 96.

by the finite' even with the restriction that this does not mean 'raising the infinite to a *qualitatively higher level of intensity* of perfection than it had before'.[42]

Lastly, Clarke has something to say on the question about suffering in God: 'I think we must have the courage to be consistent and should therefore admit in the divine consciousness something corresponding to what we would call compassion, purified of all that would be genuine imperfection. . . . Thus for God to be compassionate would not entail that he is also thereby unhappy'.[43] I am grateful for this, as for so much else that Fr Clarke has written. It is perhaps obvious that there is compassion in the risen Jesus for his brothers and sisters because he has himself experienced the worst of our sufferings. But there does not seem to be any marked tendency among those who believe in him to say that he still *suffers* in any way after winning the victory over death. Pascal in a famous passage did say so, but we are not called upon to take his words literally. In conclusion, I can only repeat that the infinite love which, according to the Christian tradition, God has for us, seems to me to be all that we can properly desire and that to require anything more, by way either of giving to him or of receiving from him, may be to go astray.

[42]Pp. 97-98.

[43]P. 100. I must not pretend that Fr Clarke and I are ultimately in agreement on the substantive issue. He recommends to us the work of Père Jean Galot, S.J., who in his book *Dieu Souffre-t-il?* (1975) argued that God must be free to make himself suffer and that revelation indicates the affirmative answer to his question. In the article to which Clarke refers us (*Nouvelle Revue Théologique*, 1979) Galot declares that it is a misuse of words to suggest that anyone can be compassionate without suffering pain. Abstractly considered, that is undeniable. But we have to use words in special ways when speaking of God, and his perfect understanding and concern are not, in my view, accompanied by distress.

Fr Clarke's concessions to the process theologians have been adopted by Ronald H. Nash in his important book, *The Concept of God* (Zondervan, 1983). In other respects it is an admirable defence of traditional positions. Nash remains hesitant on the question of God's timelessness.

V
A Neo-Whiteheadian

In the first chapter I mentioned Fr W. Norris Clarke's reference in *The Philosophical Approach to God* to writers who 'wish to push the process conception closer to the tradition by drawing out the implications of the Whiteheadian doctrine that God gives the initial subjective aim to each new actual occasion...it might be likened to an initial gift of being, as an overflow from the divine creativity'.[1] But, Clarke pointed out, this need not mean more than that God offers the subjective aim but not 'the actual energy to pursue it', and so we would still be left with the emergence out of nothing of the entity's actuality or actual power'. Now I must borrow the passage that follows:

> There is, however, another much more promising line of approach now being advanced by a number of young Neo-Whiteheadian Christian philosophers and theologians, who propose that there is a positive overflow, an actual caused influx, both from God and from the neighboring perishing entities, by which the living current of creativity is passed on before or just as the immediately preceding actual entities pass away. To back this up, appeal is made to Whitehead's too little exploited terms such as 'transitional creativity...'. The 'self-creativity' or *causa sui* aspect of the newly arriving occasion so stressed by Whitehead is in fact limited to what it does with this influx of transitional creativity, how it selects subjectively its own ways of prehending its past. It is here that the transitional creativity, not yet fully subjectivized, passes into concrescent subjective creativity.

This thesis is then illustrated by quoting from a letter

[1]P. 76.

written to Clarke by 'a young Neo-Whiteheadian theologian', Marjorie Hewitt Suchocki, in which she remarks that 'Whitehead expands on the initial aim's creative character by saying that God and the world jointly constitute the character of creativity for the initial phase of the novel concrescence'. Clarke hopes that such a 'conception of creativity as an actual causal influx...might also open the way to a theory of the radical origin of the universe out of nothing, springing from the primal influx of creativity from God alone...'.[2]

So, when Dr Suchocki's book *God-Christ-Church*[3] became available a few years later, I opened it with high hopes. But there is nothing in it, although God is referred to as 'Creator', to suggest that the strange Whiteheadian picture of a primaeval chaos, which God finds awaiting his ministrations, is being given up or even questioned. And in a useful Glossary of Process Terms at the end of the book we are told about 'transitional creativity' only that it is 'the process of influencing another's becoming'. There are, however, compensations sufficient to justify devoting a short chapter to the book. Some elements of Whitehead's system, barely touched on so far, appear in it. It makes, on the whole, agreeable reading and is free from the ill-informed invectives against 'classical theism' which have come to be associated with process thinkers. Some of its themes, although by no means unknown (as some readers might be led to suppose) to traditional theology, are here expounded with great effectiveness. And it was desirable for me to consider the views of a process thinker who is discovered, towards the end of the book, to believe in 'subjective immortality', that is, personal resurrection.

Suchocki announced her programme as follows: 'By using Whitehead's model of experience, we push toward

[2]P. 82.
[3]Published by Crossroad (New York) 1982. The subtitle is: 'A Practical Guide to Process Theology'. It can be recommended as a readable introduction to the subject, although from the nature of the case it cannot be always easy to follow.

the rewards of deepening our own vision and action in the world through theological thought'.[4] First we are asked to consider the development of an imaginary person called Catherine. We see that 'who she is takes shape through her relation to that which is external to her' and that 'just as they shape her, she shapes them'.[5] But how is one individual produced by these many influences? The answer comes: 'Unification must be a process of feeling many influences, evaluating them, and selectively interpreting them according to one's own purposes. This is creativity'.[6] That describes well the process of personal growth, but it does nothing to *account for* their unification. Then we have a picture of Catherine's pulling herself together before a moment of decision to show that 'identity is constantly being created through a series of becomings', followed immediately by the claim: 'the continuity of the self must be provided by the successiveness of instances, and not through some unchanging endurance through time'.[7] Most of us will need more than this to persuade us that a person is just a succession of instances. Then, after a chapter on the mechanics of Whitehead's cosmology, we come to a new topic: 'The interrelatedness of existence provides the structure whereby enrichment occurs; the many are for the one, and the one for the many. But this is also precisely the structure whereby sin occurs: the inescapability of relationships means that the avenues of enrichment may become avenues of destruction'.[8] The upshot is that 'The power of sin is its imprisoning nature' (that is impressively worked out) and that 'the experience of release from sin can lead to a doctrine of God'.[9] The argument which follows can be thus summed up: The awareness of sin is the recognition that a certain *power* was offered us and that we rejected it. And this leads to Whitehead's evidence for

[4] P. 5.
[5] P. 7.
[6] P. 8.
[7] P. 9.
[8] P. 22.
[9] P. 35.

God: 'The mental pole of every actual occasion is a grasp of a possibility that comes to it not simply from the past but from the future. There is real novelty in the world; the future has power. . . . If Whitehead wishes to find a source in actuality for the power of the future he must find a source not simply for one future. . .but for all possible futures whatsoever. Whitehead needs a source for possibilities *per se*. Only an existing entity, an *actual entity*, can provide such a source'.[10] Why should it not be the ultimate source of the world itself?

At this point it may be useful to recall that, in Whitehead's account, the 'mental pole' is, as Suchocki puts it, 'the grasp of possibility, the feeling for what might be the case'[11] and the physical pole, again as she puts it, is 'the beginning of the new occasion. . .a feeling of the total past. . .a feeling of otherness'[12] ('prehension' is another word for such feeling). So the proposal about introducing God into the system is supported as follows: 'The mental pole *per se* is not limited in terms of possibilities; on the contrary, a mental pole not bound by the prior restrictions of the physical pole could conceivably be infinite in possibilities. If a unique entity "began" in the mental pole and was "completed" by the physical pole, perhaps a source for possibilities could be named'.[13] In that case that mental pole and the physical pole would have changed places. Suchocki remarks that 'an actuality that begins in the mental pole cannot properly "begin" at all', because 'possibilities are non-temporal, existing eternally' and so 'an entity containing all possibilities must likewise be eternal'. When Whitehead talks about God's beginning in the mental pole, 'he is talking about the sense in which God's eternal nature is the basis for all the divine activity'.[14] That is what he means by God's 'primordial nature' (the physical

[10]P. 36.
[11]P. 20.
[12]P. 16.
[13]P. 37.
[14]P. 38.

pole, in which God 'feels' all that happens in the world, being the 'consequent' nature). It is, however, not merely allowed but emphasized as consistent with process principles that the whole original process pattern goes into reverse: 'The reversal of the dynamics of reality for one actuality in order to account for the power of possibility does not violate the model, it completes it'.[15] This seems to me singularly unconvincing. It is true that, with a little ingenuity, 'the dynamics of a physical pole, mental pole, subjective aim, concrescence and satisfaction', as Suchocki here lists them, can be made to work out in reverse order: God has satisfaction at the mental pole in his vision of the harmonized possibles, and his subjective aim, unlike that of other realities, is first for us and only secondly 'serves to direct the divine concrescence through the physical pole'.[16] But that does not show that this picture has any basis in reality, and from my point of view the whole enterprise has started in the wrong place: God fills a gap in a metaphysical construction which has been built up so far without needing him, and he then 'concresces' along with it.

We are told that 'because possibilities are harmonized within the divine nature, they are given beauty.... The very fact that it is a single reality which gives a home to possibilities means that the possibles are clothed in the value of unity, harmony and beauty' and that the fulfilment of God's aim for them 'depends upon that which is other than God, the becoming realities'. As we have had occasion to note before, it is in accordance with traditional doctrine to say that God offers us, his free creatures, at every moment what is best for us in view of the state of affairs to which our refusals of his offers have made their contributions. We are also told here: 'In the everlasting process, the consequent nature is integrated with the primordial nature in unity.... That is to say that the harmony of possibility within the primordial vision is ever more deeply intensified through God's feeling of reality

15P. 37.
16P. 39.

according to the subjective aim of harmony'.[17] That, I hardly need to add, the tradition rejects. This is the place for remarking that process theology in our time, at least in the version of it published in Europe, tends to accept Hartshorne's view that Whitehead's whole thesis about God's 'eternal objects' only causes unnecessary difficulties.

There is one more passage in Part I of this book which calls for comment. 'Ordinarily', Suchocki writes, 'God is hidden in the world'. She continues:

> Because of this hiddenness, the reality of God is inferred from experience rather than known directly from experience. Therefore we are particularly dependent upon criteria of intellectual consistency and coherence in developing formal notions of God. Does God exist? Then what we say of God must be intellectually in keeping with what we understand as existence. Otherwise, there would be an arbitrariness to our concept of God which would undercut the power of the concept, weakening its ability to address the whole of our reality. As we have seen, Whitehead follows this by insisting that the concept of God should not be an exception to existence but an exemplification of what it means to exist.[18]

It will be seen that the writer has considerable power of persuasion (enhanced, as the book proceeds, by an attractively generous personality). She is certainly being consistent here but, as I see it, on a wrong basis. It is impossible to build a sound bridge from finite to infinite by means of inference. Inference moves horizontally from one conclusion about the finite to another. Unless there is some direct contact between the human mind and God (vertically, as it were) theology is all guess work. Certainly this contact is at first, and as a rule, largely hidden. But this is not a conceptual business and, in the end, only *attention* to it will bring conviction. (In practice a good deal of argument may be required as a preliminary.) But all that is only leading up to a basic disagreement about *who* God is: I would put into reverse a sentence of Suchocki's and say that what we

17P. 40.
18P. 44.

understand as existence must be intellectually in keeping with what we say of God. And what we must say of God is that we find him 'beyond' everything that we call an 'existent'. We cannot place him in a category; there is no *description* of him. He is not an *instance* of anything. We can call him the Source of existence, but just using that capital letter will not convey what we mean to anyone who needs information. But I welcome the remark that 'without the wider frame of reference provided by philosophy, theological statements run the risk of being based only on the needs which they address'.[19]

Suchocki did not entirely reject direct experience of God, but said that he is inferred from experience rather than directly experienced. As Part II of her book proceeds, it becomes clearer that she is talking about what I have called 'direct but mediate' knowledge of God, and eventually we find: 'The whole world is touched by God, and therefore it can mediate God's presence to us'.[20] We also find a discussion of God's timeless knowledge of time as maintained by the tradition. It works up to this passage: 'It will not do to say that there is a nontemporal knowing of the temporal. Such a knowing reduces the moments of living to the celluloid frames of a motion picture, creating the illusion of movement through static instances. There is then a capturing of observed time, but the life that made it worth capturing in the first place is not thereby made present'.[21] This is a subtle form of an argument considered earlier. The heart of it is that transience is so bound up with human experience that it must be found in all true knowledge of this experience. We must say, I think, as before, that what we have to call God's timeless 'present' is incompatible with timefulness, if only because that is bound up with dissatisfactions, and that God knows our states of consciousness (they are 'before his eyes') but does not literally share them. Suchocki concludes: 'If we attempt an

[19] P. 45.
[20] P. 68.
[21] P. 72.

understanding of God based upon the dynamics of existence as process, then it will follow that God's knowledge is
precise, knowing all reality just as it knows itself. God
knows that it is raining in Chicago not "by feeling it, but
through the reality of the drops of moisture as they fall and
through the experience of wetness as the drops touch the
earth"...'.[22]

There are no further developments to detain us until we
come to Part III ('A Process Christology'). Suchocki, unlike
Schubert Ogden, for instance, accepts the distinction
between 'general' and 'special' revelation. 'Incarnation',
she writes, 'is coherent in process thought' provided that
there is 'continuity with the past', an aim for 'a full communication of the nature of God'; and 'a free conformity to
the aim, for to the degree that the recipient deviated from
the aim, to that degree incarnation would fail.... There
would have to be an assent to incarnation in every moment
of existence'.[23] Traditional theologians have nothing to
object to in this or in the account, so far as it goes, of the
New Testament witness: 'The resurrection becomes the
lens through which the story of Jesus is viewed; through
the resurrection, Jesus is seen not only as the expected
deliverer from oppression but as the manifestation of God
for us',[24] and the 'oppression' is not only that of injustice
but that of the sin which causes injustice. But after a few
admirable pages on these lines we come to something
which I find odd in the extreme. Suchocki asks the question: 'Do we fall into the problem of anthropomorphism, of
describing God in human terms so that what we are saying
of God is essentially no more than we can say about
humanity?' And she answers: 'Process Theology contributes to the resolution of the dilemma with the understanding of "actual entity" as a model for reality. Human
beings are constituted by many actual entities.... The

[22]P. 73. The passage ends: 'Every actuality that comes into existence is
felt in its entirety, as it felt itself, by God'. This seems to be panpsychism
with a vengeance.
[23]Pp. 95-96.
[24]P. 97.

description of the actual entity is more basic than the description of the human being.... The same dynamics will enter into the description of entities in a human being and entities in a puff of smoke—or the singular entity which is God...therefore by discussing God in terms of an actual entity rather than as a series of entities such as are required to constitute human beings, we can utilize the dynamics of the model to express the nature of God in non-anthropomorphic terms'.[25] But the difficulties of connecting an actual entity which is everlastingly con- crescing with other entities seems insuperable.[26] Here is another instance of a Whiteheadian thesis which has been abandoned by Hartshorne and his increasingly numerous adherents, who regard God as a 'society of occasions'.

It comes as no surprise to read: 'If God is in Jesus then God reveals through him that every sin is a sin felt by God and is therefore a sin against God, every pain is felt by God, and is therefore God's pain. The dreadful truth revealed in the crucifixion of Jesus Christ is that the world crucifies God'.[27] Suchocki goes on to say that Jesus 'most surely also reveals God through resurrection'. For on process princi- ples God's pain 'must be integrated with God's vision of harmony...resurrection *must* occur, for God *is* resurrec- tion through the power of the primordial nature'.[28] But how does God in Christ free us from a sinful past? The first answer offered is that the crucifixion shows to us God's triumph over the demonic forces so that 'we, too, can endure and look for the form of resurrection fashioned for our immediate moments'. The second answer is that 'God will lead the church to proclaim the power of God in our histories.... Jesus, by revealing the nature of God as resurrection, is the means of salvation from the forms of

[25]P. 103.

[26]Professor Neville's *Creativity and God,* referred to in note 23 to Chap- ter Three above, discusses them at length in his second chapter.

[27]Pp. 109-110. Otherwise, it is argued, God cannot give us 'the possi- bilities which can lead to our transformation' because he will not know us 'from the inside'. Is this thinkable?

[28]P. 113.

death.... The God who encounters us through the pages
of a gospel, encounters us still in the faithfulness of the
everlasting divine presence'.[29] There are many passages in
this part of the book of which all Christians should approve
and which could be very helpful to anyone. But there is
nothing in them which is special to Process Christology,
although their author naturally thinks otherwise. And
there is something that traditional Christians will find
lacking. It is not that an impoverished doctrine of God
obtrudes itself—in the passages which I have in mind there
is no sign of it. It is the relation in which, according to the
tradition, Jesus stands to the divine Word (about which
there will be something more later) that finds no mention.

In Part IV ('A Process Ecclesiology') we find Christ in
God 'illumining the actuality of the primordial nature
through the beauty of his manifestation of that nature in
our history'. The passage continues: 'Through Christ the
depths of God are touched for the world: new possibilities
for reflecting divine harmony in human history shine out
for us. The church is born'.[30] In principle (apart from
goings-on in God's 'primordial nature') that is surely a
good way of introducing the topic of the church. And we
can give a sense to the statement: 'If our future is a part of
our present identity, and if that future has been uniquely
provided through Christ, then Christ is a part of our present identity'.[31] At first we might have the impression that
the business of the church is simply 'the achievement of
love and justice' in this world. But we are told: 'In the act of
the sacrament the individual is open to Christ and his
benefits, and in this openness, receives Christ and his
benefits'.[32] The suggestion persists that to accept what is
being said is to ally oneself with process theology, whereas
it might be said with perfect propriety by a traditional
Christian. But when we read, as we do on many other

[29]Pp. 117-119.
[30]P. 130.
[31]P. 131.
[32]P. 147.

occasions: 'In a process universe, everything affects everything else',[33] it has to be remembered that this is not the platitude that it might appear to be but implies that the world and God form a single system of interlocking entities, dependent in various ways on one another. Before Part IV ends there is a curious development. A person, Suchocki declares, is neither just a 'one' nor just a 'many'; what is needed to integrate them is 'creativity' and these three terms are interdependent. Couldn't it be possible, she asks, 'that these three basic terms might be used by God as different routes to lead us into the realization of harmony in our own existence?'[34] So, in addition to monotheism, secular humanism with its many finite values and Buddhism (insofar as emphasizing creativity) might be God-directed. 'Couldn't we experience a world community of religions as a unity created through diversity and love? Won't love bind us into a gladness at the differences and at the samenesses that are cradled within those differences?'[35] It may be necessary to point out that belief in Christ does not require us to deny that either Buddhists or conscientious humanists may be worshipping, although they do not know it, the one true God.

Part V ('A Process Eschatology'), at the end of its five chapters (on the Kingdom and the Gospel), presents us with a most astonishing claim. In connection with 'the double focus of time and eternity' which we have to employ in dealing with the scriptural imagery of the Kingdom of God, we find the following passage: 'Among the unique contributions of process thought is that the peculiar metaphysics of the system allow formulations of a contemporary vision of God that highlights the viability of both dimensions, and that indicates the way in which both dimensions affect each other. The temporal work toward the Kingdom of God is not separate from the eternal establishment of the Kingdom; likewise, the eternal establish-

[33]P. 149.
[34]P. 154.
[35]P. 160.

ment of the Kingdom affects the possibilities for ways in which to live justly and with love'.[36] Process theology does indeed bring the two dimensions together in its own peculiar way, which involves the reducing of God's timelessness to everlastingness. But the suggestion that traditional thought knows nothing of 'realized eschatology' is breathtaking. Then that is more than compensated for by the discovery that Suchocki's belief in personal resurrection, already hinted at several times, is clear and definite: 'Future life must be one wherein there is an ultimate attainment of well-being through the process of resurrection and judgment... divine power enacts the fulfilment of the ever-repeated promise of justice.... Christians frequently fail to see the tremendous issue of justice that stands or falls on the reality of the resurrection'.[37] One may hope that this will encourage other process thinkers to reach the same conclusion. 'Early church theologians', Suchocki writes, 'expressed the resurrection as a promotion into God and a participation in God. Process theology must reiterate these sensitivities, and suggest that resurrection is a rebirth of ourselves in God through the divine feeling'.[38] A dozen pages follow, in explanation of this, much more complicated than any other part of the book, which must detain us for some time.

'To feel the other', we are told, 'is to be in touch with its feelings of itself...no subject can feel the totality of another subject's feelings on the finite level.... This does not hold true with regard to God's feelings of the world... all actuality whatsoever can be incorporated into God's primordial experience of unity...the flow of feeling that takes place as God prehends the other is a flow of the full subjectivity of the other into the full subjectivity of God. ... Mortal nature becomes immortal; sin and death have no place in this transformation of our natures.... God feels all subjectivities in the process vision. Transforma-

[36]Pp. 174-175.
[37]Pp. 176-177.
[38]P. 179.

tion is not restricted to humanity but must be extended to the whole universe'.[39] These sentences sum up, it seems to me, some three pages. The last of them, as it stands, is part of traditional doctrine, which has, however, nothing to say about *how* God recreates his world, just as it has nothing to say about *how* he created it in the first place. And I must here confess that I never know quite what to make of these 'feelings' which are enjoyed by ourselves, the world around us, and God. We need not go into the ensuing technical argument to prove that 'the subjectivities that are resurrected in God are no longer definable in terms of material togetherness'. But this leads to another technical argument to deal with the question: How can this subject resurrected in God continue to experience anything at all? For in process philosophy a subject once completed through 'concrescence' and 'satisfaction' cannot be added to, so how can it experience transformation in God? The answer turns first to God's feeling, which 'constitutes a reversal of the dynamics of becoming, analogous to God's own reversal in moving from the eternity of the primordial pole toward the everlastingness of the consequent pole and the integration of the two'. The point is that 'God feels the finite subject's satisfaction and consequently the concrescence' so that 'the resurrected subjectivity is retained in reversal of its finite state, and so, when it comes, as it were, to itself in God it is "always more than itself" '. It moves away from the solitude of satisfaction into the fullness of God's own feeling'.[40] Such are the complications, for a process thinker, in facing the question of what some of us, less encumbered, would call simply an 'awareness' of God.

What follows about 'judgment and transformation' comes to something much like the traditional doctrine of purgatory. We are to suppose that a woman has been unjustly condemned and executed. God has 'co-experienced' every moment of her existence, and now it is 'through

[39]Pp. 179-181.
[40]Pp. 182-183.

God's concrescence that her own concrescence is re-
enacted'. She 'would feel herself in God with the co-
presence of God's feeling with her'. But 'God's feeling of
the completed occasion' (of which he is in every case 'the
source and destiny') will include a knowledge of 'what that
occasion could have been, given the initial aim' (God's
offer). The woman 'knows herself as she would have been,
and as she is'. And would she not have in God 'not only the
awareness of the self from the divine perspective, but an
awareness of the self as others had experienced the self?
Moreover she would not only experience the momentary
judgment of a particular instant but also a composite
judgment concerning her total being...'. [41] We now turn
to the unjust judge. He will have analogous experiences.
He 'will experience God's feeling of her as a judgment of
wrath against himself for what might have been...'. I can
make something of that. It is when process is described as it
affects God that I have to dissent fundamentally: 'It is a
movement into integration, whereby the many feelings in
the consequent nature are brought into increasing modes
of unity...pulled toward the vortex of God, where the
many are together in the unfathomable depths of unity
and justice'. [42] It is not simply that the picture of a changing
God is unacceptable. So far as I can see, God's life, in that
account, consists only in organizing possibilities of unity,
beauty, and holiness, and contemplating the results. I come
back to the question: has God, apart from the world and
what he does with it, no life *of his own*? It would seem not.
For at the end of the chapter which we have just been
considering, there is this passage: 'Differentiation remains
in the primordial depths of God, but a differentiation that
is divinely sustained as the most fitting actuality of unity,
beauty, holiness: the kingdom of God which is *the kingdom in
God which is God*'. [43] The following chapter ('The Kingdom of
God') is about present tasks ('political liberation, black lib-

[41]Pp. 183-185.
[42]P. 187.
[43]P. 190 (my italics).

eration, feminist liberation, and the underlying root of all three, which is economic liberation, are the edges of the kingdom as the church pushes toward new forms of realizing the image of God in society').[44] The final chapter ('Thy Kingdom Come') is about how prayer empowers us for these tasks. There is a conclusion ('God for us: Trinity') which might seem to offer some hope. But 'Trinity', we are told, just means God's presence, wisdom and power: 'the magnitude of the divine power that accomplishes the vision of the divine wisdom, all within the everlasting unity of presence.'[45] What it means for the tradition is a topic touched on in earlier chapters, which will be further discussed in the next one.

[44]P. 197.
[45]P. 216.

VI
A Traditional Viewpoint

Towards the end of the first chapter I said that the topic of religious experience would be taken up again in the final one and that Father Dermot Lane's *The Experience of God* would be discussed in further detail. 'Religious experience' is an expression which sounds disagreeable in most people's ears. It suggests peculiar psychological states which cannot be regarded as evidence for anything except an emotional temperament and which commonly lead to odd notions and tiresome behaviour. But if knowing, awareness, is an experience, and if an awareness of God proves to be indispensable for an intellectually respectable theology, as well as being a fact which can be unearthed from ordinary human experience, then a rejection of religious experience will seem to be a prejudice of which many people still need to be disabused. Among Catholics there have been special reasons for the prevalence of such a prejudice. At the beginning of this century Catholic theology was at a low ebb: the faith of the Church seemed almost to be reduced to the faith of its pastors, who had received it from their predecessors and through them from the Apostles—nobody, since the Apostles, had the truth at first hand. This, together with a generally obscurantist attitude on the part of the authorities, made thinking Catholics realize that something had to be done. And this resulted in what came to be called 'The Modernist Crisis'. Some of these people were led to attack genuinely traditional beliefs, and in 1907 Pope Pius X published an encyclical which set off a persecution of many blameless thinkers and nipped in the bud many promising developments in theology which came to fruition only with Vatican II some twenty years ago. Many Catholics would still say that you can prove the existence of God but that you cannot at all *know* him this side of the grave—you can only trust his promises. But that attitude of mind is dying out. Father Lane puts it like this:

> One of the most significant developments in Christian theology in this century has been the recovery of experience as an integral element in the exercise of theology. This development is especially remarkable in Catholic theology in view of the fact that there was something of a magisterial ban against the use of experience in theology.... By way of reaction against Modernism, Catholic theology deliberately isolated itself from historical, social, scientific, and cultural developments. Barriers were erected between life and theology.... The argument from authority assumed absolute significance. This kind of apartheid was inconsistent with the witness of the theological tradition.[1]

It is not surprising, then, that the founders of process theology found little to approve of in the Catholic theology of their time. But it is surprising that their successors have shown so little interest in its later developments.[2]

The first half of this century is not, however, the only period in which there has been a general distrust of religious experience understood as an experience of God himself. Aquinas's view that the natural reason could have no knowledge of *who* God is would not have mattered so much if he had been willing to refer to union with God in the life of faith as a properly cognitive one as well as one of love: here he makes love move ahead of knowledge, contrary to his general principle that 'nothing is willed unless it is first known'. This played into the hands of those who maintained that 'mysticism' or experiential knowledge of God

---

[1]*The Experience of God*, p. 5.

[2]Schubert Ogden, however, uses for the epigraph of *The Reality of God* a passage from *The Discovery of God*, the translation of Henri de Lubac's book *Sur les Chemins de Dieu*, in which he develops the theme of God's accessibility for the human mind.

was something very special for very special people, not for the faithful in general. Some fifty years ago Garrigou-Lagrange established conclusively that the genuinely traditional view is that Christian mysticism is simply the normal development of faith[3] (which does not mean that it is in fact very commonly to be met with), from which it follows that faith itself must contain a mystical element. But this has been slow to penetrate the general consciousness of the faithful, for the suspicion of mysticism had become deeply embedded ever since the disastrous dispute between Bossuet and Fénelon in the seventeenth century. Then there was the spirit of the time to discourage the acceptance of any conscious communion with the transcendent; rationalism in the eighteenth century, typified by Kant's rejection of intuitive awareness, the spreading of agnosticism in the nineteenth and of scepticism in our own. There was once a time when to be a Christian was to be, as a matter of course, both a theologian and a 'mystic'.

In the last forty years or so, and especially since Vatican II, there has been a gradual return among Catholic theologians to the early medieval and patristic tradition about Christian faith, called 'supernatural' to distinguish it from a bare acceptance of God's existence. One of the features of process theology is a disavowal of 'supernaturalism'. We must therefore look more closely at this vitally important topic of faith before entering upon a further discussion of its development into mysticism. This topic has been dealt with by Father Henri Bouillard, S.J. more clearly and authoritatively than by any other writer known to me. So I shall now quote from the English translation of his

[3]The English translation of his book, *Christian Perfection and Contemplation* (London and St Louis) was published in 1937. The writer's 'high Thomism' should not be allowed to prejudice the reader against the valid historical and theological argument of the book. He makes clear that 'mysticism', in its proper Christian sense, has no necessary connection with extraordinary phenomena such as levitations. What it aims at is not some merely psychological state but union with God, which involves subordinating all other interests to interest in him and the coming of his Kingdom.

Logique de la Foi[4] some passages which will indicate, I hope, a position which will seem meaningful and consistent. The basis of it is made clear in the following words:

> God reveals himself to each of us in the heart of the act of faith which he determines and evokes. Our consciousness of this revelation has the quality of a direct, personal intuition; it is an intimate experience, a supernatural perception analogous to mystical knowledge. Today this is admitted by many theologians. And it is this experience of God that constitutes the sure basis of our faith.[5]

This is a far cry from the widespread notion that by 'faith' is meant the blind acceptance of formulas from the accredited ecclesiastical authorities. A few lines below, after emphasizing that 'the divine revelation brings conviction with it' and that 'our certitude in its regard comes from our direct apprehension of it', Bouillard is equally emphatic that this apprehension occurs in a medium:

> Knowledge of God by faith consists in recognizing him in the historical signs of his actual revelation. Whoever says revelation says manifestation by signs. By signs we mean not alone miracles of the physical or moral order but the totality of divine action that constitutes the history of salvation.... The sign of signs is the human reality of Jesus Christ.

In other words, it is a prerequisite for faith that one should be acquainted in some way with the historical phenomenon of Christianity—obviously, for no one could be converted instantaneously to a religion about which he had heard nothing. But, further, what must be eventually encountered is the man Jesus as the revelation of God; there must be a conviction that he has risen from the dead

---

[4]*The Logic of Faith,* (Gill, Logos Books, 1967). A warning is needed that this translation is not only sometimes infelicitous but also not always as accurate as it is in the passages quoted.

[5]P. 16. 'Determines' here means that faith is God's gift. Bouillard emphasizes that the act of faith, the acceptance of the gift, is 'an act of perfectly free choice'.

as Son of God, an awareness of him as more than man.
Bouillard continues:

> But note that these signs are not the middle term in a line of
> reasoning that would inevitably lead to the conclusion that
> God has actually revealed himself. They are the place of junc-
> ture in which we experience the transparency (so to speak) in
> which we perceive the revelation God is making to us. . . . But
> while we read the revelation in the signs, our perception of it
> is nonetheless obscure.[6]

In other words, it is as if it percolated through the signs or
pervaded them. To perceive it, one must be willing to
attend to it, to open oneself to it. It will be obvious that
reason can prepare one for faith on this account. The fact
of God's revelation cannot be certified but can be suggested by logical processes. Bouillard now proceeds to
claim that faith gives the answer to another question
which is raised by our natural powers of thought. Here he
is following Maurice Blondel, whose famous book, *L'Action*
(1893), has exercised a profound influence on French theological thought and thus on that of Vatican II:

> . . . The signs would have no meaning for anyone if the
> mystery they were supposed to make known had no intrinsic
> relation to human existence. But, as it happens, their purpose
> is to impress on us that communion with God is our super-
> natural end. . . . We must therefore show that Christian faith
> is the indispensable condition for the fulfilment of our human
> destiny. No apologetic is of any value that does not deal
> somehow or other with this point. It would be useless to
> enumerate miracles and prodigious events if the Christian
> phenomenon of which they form part could not be convinc-
> ingly established as the answer to the question of our exis-
> tence. . . . When it has been shown what our relationship to
> the Absolute is, and what it ought to be, it remains to demon-
> strate that Christianity is the historical definition of that
> relationship. . . . I do not think anyone has improved on Blon-
> del's definition of what apologetics ought to be in our contem-
> porary world.[7]

[6] P. 17.
[7] Pp. 18, 23, 25, 29.

This leads to the question about a 'philosophical moment' in the recognition of God as revealing himself to us in Christ. Bouillard replies to the rejection of it by Karl Barth, the most famous theologian of the Reform in our century:

> Barth states that knowledge of God by faith presupposes the operation, the *event*, of divine grace. . . . We agree. We would add, however, that knowledge by faith presupposes natural knowledge of God in the subject; it need not be mentally formulated, but it must be capable of formulation. . . . How could we discern the action of God. . . if our spiritual being did not possess the power of knowing God, if the Absolute, whose presence is perceptible in our heart of hearts, bore no relation to the God of whom the Bible speaks?[8]

It is, I suppose, conceivable that someone might have lived so subhuman an existence that God's revelation in Christ might seem to him altogether dissociated from his previous experience. But he would have to recognize that it is *God* who is summoning *before* (not in time but in logic) he could accept his revelation in Christ.

The 'supernatural' knowledge, the awareness of faith, as one may call it, is the beginning of a union with God which is something far more intimate than knowledge at the 'natural' or philosophical level. For traditional Christians, it contains, in germ, all theology. The doctrinal formulations eventually worked out try to safeguard the richness implicit in the original Christian experience. (St Paul's letters reveal to us how the first generation of Christians spoke of the Father, the Son, and the Spirit.) It is a commonplace to say that the Christian truths can be understood only in the 'light' of faith, only through 'grace'. But what do these words mean? Here I must quote Bouillard once again:

> The determining factor in believing is described as the light of grace, as the Holy Spirit shedding his light upon our souls. . . . But this is sometimes interpreted too imaginatively, as if man were faced with a revelation independent of all perception, to

discern and accept which he would be favoured with a supernatural light, which would let him see the revelation. . . . The
divine light in the soul is nothing other than that of the
revelation received. The Word that God pronounces in Jesus
reaches the believer's soul through the medium of the Holy
Spirit. And the light of faith is this very Word insofar as it is
apprehended by the believer.[9]

This fits in with the view, which is becoming better known
today, that the human mind of Jesus Christ is the original
recipient of that revelation which he himself *is*, as he
becomes conscious of his mission and of the definitive role
which he has to play in the working out of God's supreme
purpose for us. It is in him that we are united with the
Father. So *he* is the Church's teacher. St Paul says: 'We
have the mind of Christ'. It is the contemplation of the
risen Christ at work in his Church that is the mainspring
of all theology. This contemplation is at the root of all
living faith. It may appear first in consciousness only as a
settled conviction that Christ is the Word of God or (as St
John says) that he is the Way, the Truth, and the Life. But
the conviction is meant to grow, to become more luminous.

This theme has been worked out most convincingly for
our time, it seems to me, by Father Louis Bouyer of the
Oratory, in his *Introduction to Spirituality*.[10] He refers to mysticism 'in its modern, specifically spiritual meaning' as 'the
full and personal apprehension on the part of the Christian
of what is proclaimed by the divine Word and given to us in
the sacraments: the fullness of the new life, the divine life
which we find in Christ who died and rose again'. He calls
it, echoing Garrigou-Lagrange, 'the normal development
of Christian perfection' and reaches the conclusion that
'the first act of charity springing from faith in the divine
Word, faith nourished by the sacraments, contains in germ
the whole of mysticism'.[11] It is not a 'Greek contamination'

[9]P. 16.
[10]The translation (published by Desclée, New York) of his *Introduction à
la Vie Spirituelle*.
[11]Pp. 302-303.

of Christianity but 'specifically Christian (biblical and Jewish in the first place)...an eminently personal knowledge...which is at the same time a union and a conformation...it is a knowledge which can and ought in its own way to become as real as, more real than, the knowledge of sense-presented realities...it is a vision insofar as it is a knowledge without intermediary, in which we know God by his own presence and his own activity in us'.[12] But it is not the beatific (heavenly) vision, for that is impossible so long as we are in the present body.

Until quite recently it was usual for children in our society to accept the religion of their parents, although often in a merely nominal way. It is now becoming less and less usual. Eventually, it might seem, passive acceptance of religion will die out. The advantage of this, for a religion which has real life in it, is that there will be no longer any merely nominal adherents to lower standards which put people off. When a large and lax community becomes smaller, it can be on the way to becoming large and flourishing. What makes such a community flourish is, fundamentally, a loving awareness of God (that is, mysticism), as historians who are not hostile to religion seem to agree. What is needed, then, is encouragement to believe that God is actively present to the human mind, waiting (as it were) for his activity to be recognized. But if it is to become something directly known, *realized* instead of being merely admitted as a fact, it must be *attended to* in favourable conditions, not easy to come by for most people today. A certain training is necessary, and the help of others may be required. God refuses his grace to no one who obeys the dictates of his conscience, Christian or non-Christian, as Vatican II has emphasized. But the faith that begins with the acceptance of God's grace (that is, of his love) is not Christian faith until Jesus Christ is seen to be God's revelation of himself and acknowledged as such. All grace comes to man through Christ, but it is not until it is known to do so that it can bring him, so far as this world is concerned,

[12]Pp. 264, 299.

into the richer knowledge of the Christian society; that is the traditional standpoint.[13]

At this point I shall return to Lane's book *The Experience of God* and consider what he says there about mysticism. 'For most people', he writes, 'it means some kind of direct and intimate union with the presence of God'. He continues:

> The obvious temptation is to dismiss this kind of religious outlook as somewhat fanciful. However, a certain caution is called for here. It is at least possible that an individual, after undergoing many rich religious experiences, might momentarily disregard the medium disclosing the religious dimension of life and thus focus exclusively, *though darkly*, on the transcendent. Such is conceivable in the lives of those who are particularly advanced and mature in the ways of the Lord...it acts as a useful corrective to those who concentrate too much on the medium in religious experience to the neglect of personal communion with God which is the goal of all religious experience.... However, mysticism should not be presented as the principal experiential point of contact with God.[14]

This passage seems to me to blow hot and cold alternately in a confusing way. As a whole it may seem to be contradicting most of what I have been saying about mysticism. But the difference between us is to a considerable extent about the meaning which should be given to the word 'mysticism'. Lane's view of this I venture to regard as outmoded. But there does seem to be a certain difference between us about the more fundamental question of the meaning which should be given to 'religious experience'. He disapproves, we have to conclude, of any attempt to

[13]The importance of making this restriction has been brought home to me by Professor Huw Owen. It seems to be overlooked by Karl Rahner. 'Anonymous theist' makes sense because those so described are, though unwittingly, in effective contact with God; 'anonymous Christian' does not make sense with reference to those who have not recognized the Lordship of the risen Jesus and live by his life. This is not to deny that many non-Christians may be holier here and now than many Christians nor to suggest that they will be disadvantaged hereafter.

[14]P. 18.

'disregard the medium' except for very special people. It is true that, as he also says here, 'most mystics warn' against supposing that the medium can be expected to disappear altogether, that we can 'focus exclusively' on the divine presence. But that is not to say that we cannot focus on it at all unless we are 'particularly advanced and mature'. And, to repeat, it seems a matter of extreme importance to encourage people to focus on it, though without expecting that they will have ecstatic experiences. What they may hope to have if they persevere and follow their own lights consistently is religious *conviction*. Lane has rightly rejected any idea of 'direct and immediate contact with the sacred',[15] but goes on to say that 'many theologians today talk about the "mediated immediacy" of God to the human person'.[16] He seems not to be aware that 'direct but mediated' is another formula in use and surely a more satisfactory one. A knowledge which cannot be called direct can hardly be called an *experience* of anything. He also proposes the formula that 'God can be known through all the experiences and knowledge of the human subject',[17] and when he says that 'we begin to experience God...not as a thing of value but as the ground of all valuing, not as a being before us, but as the source of all beings',[18] agreement becomes substantial. Although the mind's experience of God in its experience of *itself* is overlooked in Lane's account, it should do much good.

[15]P. 14. God is mediated, if by nothing else, by his activity in and upon the mind of the subject.

[16]P. 16. Karl Rahner, for instance, who has written: 'the devout Christian of the future will either be a "mystic", one who has "experienced" something, or he will not be anything at all', (*Theological Investigations*, vol. vii, published by Darton Longman and Todd, p. 15, illogically expressed in this translation, but the meaning will not be in doubt).

[17]P. 15. Lane adds: 'With Aquinas we would want to hold that God is known implicitly from the outset in all our experiences'. Copleston (*Aquinas*, p. 256) asks: 'What is meant by implicit knowledge in this connection...? Does it mean simply that though one does not know one is capable of knowing? And, if it means more than this, how can it be reconciled with other express statements of Aquinas?'

[18]P. 19.

To speak, then, in Christian language of a 'supernatural life' is to speak of the relationship in which a Christian stands to God 'in Christ', as St Paul so often puts it. To say that man has a 'supernatural end' is simply to say that union with God is what he has been made for, a union which can be entered upon in the present life and brought in the next to its definitive form. Nature is *for* grace, God's gift of knowing and loving him. It cannot be received passively, but must be consented to without conditions. Even this consent, which is at the time the first act of 'supernatural' love, is empowered by God and is indeed itself his gift, according to the most constant tradition of Christian thinking. It is possible for man to close himself against it out of pride or fear of the consequences, for love cannot be forced on anyone, even when the love is divine. This conclusion is profoundly mysterious, but it is recommended to us by our own experience. And without it the problem of evil threatens to contradict belief in God. God's world (not, I have suggested, one of innumerable possible worlds) is offered the highest goods, and when these are refused, is subject, inevitably, to the greatest disasters.

So nature is the sphere of necessity, grace the sphere of the freedom for which man has been created. He moves out of necessity, what he is born with, to a life of love. If he is inevitably a chooser, freedom is offered to his choice in the positive sense in which it means the breaking down of barriers, fulfilment. The will of God, as St Paul says, is man's sanctification, and that is why, in Dante's famous words, it is his peace. As Blondel puts it, at the end of *L'Action*, he finds himself, when all else has failed, seeking an answer to a need which has now wholly engrossed him. One thing, which means everything to him, is now necessary, and it is inaccessible. He has no power over it, for it is, in Pascal's words, 'of another order, supernatural'; he can only submit himself to it. And at that point God takes him over. Unless the relationship between God and man is recognized as the meaning of the 'supernatural' the word will naturally suggest, as it does to process theologians, that man's life is being split into two discordant parts. And

this danger was intensified by theologians who spoke of a
'super-nature' as something external added to nature,
something (it was easy to infer) that it could do well
enough without. Grace is not just added to nature—nature
itself is graced. This has been made abundantly clear by
Father Henri de Lubac, S.J., now a Cardinal, one of the
most influential theologians of Vatican II and, in the eyes
of some, the greatest theologian of his time.[19]

In his book on the Apostles' Creed, de Lubac writes that
it is 'the mystery of the divine Trinity that this creed
teaches us above all else'; it is also perhaps the mystery that
is most often misconstrued, even by Christians, and the
notion of a theological mystery is repugnant to most
process theologians. De Lubac goes on: 'Indeed our faith
consists in this mystery. It is for us light and life. However,
it must be clearly recognized that it is not always found
easy to understand...'.[20] Later on, he writes that 'the
revelation of the Trinitarian mystery has turned the world
upside down...in giving man's mind a new depth which he
can never finish exploring...a mystery of total transcendence, and that is just why it can penetrate us totally'.[21] On
the next page he writes of 'the perfect circumincession of
love' and comments:

> If we can realize that the God who speaks to us and wishes to
> bind our destiny to his own has in himself an eternal knowl-
> edge of himself, a dialogue which can be extended beyond
> himself, a vital movement with which we can be associated—
> if, without a philosophical education, we can resist those who
> tell us that the ultimate stuff of being is matter, it is because
> the mystery of the Trinity has opened to us an entirely new
> perspective: the ultimate stuff of being is communion. If we
> can surmount all the crises which lead us to despair of the
> human adventure, it is because, through the revelation of this
> mystery, we know that we are loved. And by the same token
> we learn what the most clear-sighted of men have been led to

[19]His *Surnaturel* was published by Aubier in 1946; his *Petite Catéchèse sur
Nature et Grace* (Fayard), with acknowledgments to Blondel, in 1980.
[20]*La Foi Chrétienne*, (Aubier, 2nd ed., 1970), p. 10.
[21]Pp. 12-13.

doubt, that we ourselves can love, that we have been made capable of it by the communication of the divine life, of that life which is love.

These are the accents of conviction. The passages quoted come from the Preface, in which two further points are now made. First, although 'the mystery of the Trinity was not revealed to us in itself, but in the activity of the Trinity *ad extra*, its historical salvific activity, it is nevertheless true that the purpose of this activity is, even now, our discernment of the Trinity itself in its own reality— although always in mystery, *in umbris et imaginibus'*. The second point is that this mystery, 'which illuminates the mystery of human existence, is wholly contained in the mystery of Christ.... Its starting point is in the earliest formulas of the Christian faith, which are the Christic formulas'.

Something more must now be said about the 'circumincession', mentioned already in connection with Professor Keith Ward's rejection of any notion of the Trinity as a *society*. In the passage to which I there referred in Father Bouyer's *Le Consolateur*, it is shown that, when St Thomas Aquinas talks about 'relations of subsistence', what he means is that Father, Son, and Spirit are identical with the 'divine essence' as relations of person to person, persons in relation. The passage continues: 'Either this is saying nothing at all, expressing only a contradiction in terms ...or else it means that the essence of God is precisely to exist in persons who are distinct but inseparable, unthinkable except in their reciprocal relations'. This interdependence rules out all objections on the score of an alleged illogicality. The divine 'nature' is not *shared equally* by three persons who are nevertheless only one God but is *constituted* by them. And to say that the divine Persons are bound up with one another in a completely unflawed love is to say something that is meaningful, even if it is thought to be an ideal that is unrealizable in fact. The contributor of the article on the doctrine of the Trinity and of that on Tritheism in *A Dictionary of Christian Theology* (1969) takes seriously Karl Barth's charge of tritheism against 'modern pluralist doctrines which appeal to the social analogy', but tritheism is incompatible with finding in the Trinity the absolute archetype of interdependence. The same contributor in the article on Coinherence (that is, circumincession) writes of it as 'the mutual indwelling or interpenetration of the three Persons of the Trinity whereby one is as invariably in the other as they are in the one.... Each person belongs to the others'. Isn't this the best way of 'pointing to' the perfection of love? Nothing could be further from the truth than the complaint of process thinkers that the God of traditional theology is 'static'. The divine Persons are precisely 'ecstatic' in an eternal activity.[22]

Process thinkers regard their metaphysical system as accounting for all the facts in a rational way. They are therefore opposed not only to 'supernaturalism' in general and to 'mysteries' (supposed to be sheer incomprehensibilities) but also to the arbitrariness (as they see it) of God's arrangements as propounded by traditional theologians. They have some excuse in the matter of God's freedom in creating, as I have granted, and in considering some popular presentations of his plans for us. It must be borne in mind that such presentations are open necessarily to such objections. Without the sort of analysis with which most people's minds are not trained to cope, one cannot give

---

[22]When it is said that Christian mysticism is Trinitarian, what may be meant is not that there is a vision of any kind but in some measure a *realization* of the mystery. St Ignatius of Loyola, however, 'seemed to see the Holy Trinity under the form of three notes played on the clavichord' (quoted from his autobiography in L. Cognet, *Histoire de la Spiritualité Chrétienne*, vol. 3. p. 17), a musical phrase being a unity of notes in interdependence. Cognet says also, in reference to St Teresa of Avila, that 'the experience which occurs when her soul reaches its true centre is essentially Trinitarian: the soul finds there both the mystery of the life of the divine persons and their indwelling in it' (*op. cit.*, p. 97). He goes on to say, perhaps surprisingly: 'That seems to have been the final stage for Teresa: in her descriptions there is nothing to indicate clearly a grasp of the Unity, beyond the Trinity of the Persons'. Perhaps 'interdependence' was not a word that she knew.

plausible answers to questions about why God did this or did not do that. But something may be said here in general terms to process thinkers about the propriety of a historical revelation. In the first place, the advent of Jesus Christ does not have to be regarded as a stratagem devised to deal with the world's sinful state. It is an accepted Christian view—probably that of most Catholic theologians today— that the Incarnation was not thought up as an emergency measure but was the point to which the world was destined to move (at the time most fitting for it), the beginning of a fresh development which the sins of men might indeed retard or impair but which could not fail to take place and to achieve (in principle) its goal, the union of the human race with the Father through the Son and in the Holy Spirit. As I had occasion to remark earlier, there must always be the hazard of our inevitable choice either to accept God or to reject him, but nothing could prevent the divine Son's perfect (and thus sinless) human expression from fulfiling his mission by living out a perfect human life and so submitting to a cruel and ignominious death, so that he might then be the Lord of life, empowered to unite his brothers and sisters with the Father by their sharing in his own risen life. This may seem to some a fantastic picture, but it has at least a grandeur not unworthy of the God whose best name is Love.

Since process thinkers accept that God offers what is best for his world at every moment, they must also accept that we cannot hope to understand 'the workings of his mind'. It is perhaps less misleading to talk of absolute goodness reacting to all our circumstances in his own omniscient way. It is intelligible that the world should be a developing one: there is a special sort of beauty about the evolutionary process which sin has not wholly destroyed. But there is also something baffling about it. There must be some reason for the vast expanses of the universe, which some have found terrifying, but we cannot expect to discover what it is (there may be so much that no telescope could reveal). Unless we are to give up the problem of human existence or deny that there is one, we must accept the God who will always remain profoundly mysterious to us. It is the verdict of Christian experience down the ages, perhaps of all experience that deserves to be called religious, that God is both the wholly other and at the same time, in Augustine's (on the face of it) nonsensical words, 'closer to us than we are to ourselves'. This is the basic fact from which Christians have to start. It should not be surprising, then, if they are led to make further statements which seem to others paradoxical or simply absurd. This is the case, in particular, for the ascription to God of time-lessness and impassibility, which, as we have seen, has given so much offence.

That is one of the two topics on which there is still something to add or to reemphasize in conclusion. In our experience time and duration are bound up together. But God, I hold, must be said to endure but not to be in time. He has the positivity that goes with enduring but not the incompleteness that goes with time. This does not mean that his enduring is to be imagined as reduced to a point. It is not to be imagined at all. If I call his knowledge an all-embracing one, I must add at once that this is not to be taken in a spatial sense. There can be no proof of this: the truth of it must be *seen*. We cannot comprehend it; but then we cannot comprehend ourselves. The realization of that may help us to appreciate better our own limitations and to recognize that we know very little even about those things which we can be said to know. We know that they are *there*, we register their effects upon ourselves, and that is all. It is the same, in principle, with our knowledge of God: we are largely ignorant of him. Yet the knowledge which we have of him, despite its severe limitations, is knowledge of a far more intimate, though far less obvious, kind than the knowledge of the world around us and its inhabitants. It does not operate in terms of sense-presented objects. Louis Lavelle has written: 'There is nothing more ambiguous than the rule which bids us live for the moment; for that can mean either thinking only of the passing event or never losing touch with the eternal act which we rediscover in every passing event, always the same and always new'.[23] On the other hand, the more we keep in touch with the 'eternal act', the more we realize that there is so much about it which we do not know at all. A timeless knowledge of what is future for us is quite beyond our grasp, but this does not entitle us to write it off as an absurdity. It does not make our time unreal, but it does make it unthinkable without eternity to support it. It is a mark of our incompleteness in which the completeness, the absoluteness, of God is made known to us. It is the conviction of this absoluteness that makes traditional theologians maintain God's impassibility. He cannot be damaged by his creatures in any way. Pain, suffering and distress, unlike generous concern, can mean only a sort of malfunctioning, even if it arises, as it does in ourselves, through a natural sympathy with others; therefore God cannot share it with us. If it is possible for someone to reject God fully and finally, how can he not be saddened? If there is anything to be said about this, it would be, I suppose, that there would be nothing left in such a person for God to love.

The second topic on which there are a few words to add is the present state of the philosophy of religion in the English-speaking countries. There is a great and growing interest in it. But an antimetaphysical bias in the universities, although it has been gradually lessening for some twenty years or more, is still very strong. There is very little support for the claim made in this book that we, all of us, can find God acting upon our own minds if we take the trouble to look for him. But on the continent of Europe there have been and are many writers who belong to this Augustinian tradition of which the chief exponent in the thirteenth century was St Bonaventure[24] and the most important, I believe, for the present time is Maurice Blondel[25]—hardly known among us except through the

[23]*Du Temps de L'Eternité*, p. 411.

[24]On this tradition section 15 of John Baillie's *Our Knowledge of God* (chapter 2) and chapter 1 of J. V. Langmead Casserley's *The Christian in Philosophy* will be found useful.

[25]The only translations of Blondel in English are of two short works,

works of those French writers whom he has so greatly influenced (de Lubac, in particular, and also Gabriel Marcel). Since the revival of Thomism at the end of the last century, which has removed so many misunderstandings (not, however, in all quarters) about traditional thinking, the older tradition has been very largely ignored. I hope not to have offended any of my Thomist friends by my disagreement with certain Thomist positions.[26] If any of them should be roused to a defence of these positions, I shall hope to learn from him. And I must repeat that despite my fundamental disagreements with the process theologians I am grateful to them for what they have taught me.

The Letter on Apologetics and *History and Dogma,* published by the Harvill Press twenty years ago (under the general title of *Maurice Blondel*) with introductions and notes by the translators, Alexander Dru and myself. For some general account of his position I am reduced to referring to the fifth chapter of my *The Absolute and the Atonement,* (Allen and Unwin, 1971). I have made some use of this book in the present chapter.

[26]They may find some excuse for my complaints about the way in which some Thomists treat of 'being' in an article 'Process Theology: A Response to Criticism' by Norman Pittenger, in which he writes of 'creativity' that it 'serves in Process Thought, especially in that of Whitehead, much the same purpose as the concept of "being" does in the Thomist Scholastic scheme', (*The Expository Times,* xcii, p. 271).

Names of Authors